Cryptocurrency

The Top Scalping And Day Trading Strategies For Cryptocurrencies

(Global Economic Analysis Of The Cryptocurrency Potential)

Neville Holden

TABLE OF CONTENT

What Is Cryptocurrency? 1

Variety Of Cryptocurrencies 27

The Growth Of Additional Cryptocurrencies ... 38

The Adoption Of Cryptocurrency By The Masses 40

List Of Suggested Cryptocurrency Ventures For Profitable Investment 60

Various Crypto Currencies And Choosing The Best 81

Mining For Consensus In A Trustless Network 113

Financial Indicators 126

The Prospects For Cryptocurrency 137

Investments In Distributed Video Streaming 142

Smart Contract Cryptocurrency Investment 160

What Is Cryptocurrency?

Any currency that can be used digitally is referred to as cryptocurrency. It is protected with cryptography, which prevents forgery. The most important and compelling feature of cryptocurrencies is that they are not issued by a central authority, which protects them from government interference and manipulation.

Cryptocurrency is a digital payment system that does not rely on institutions to verify transactions. It is a shared infrastructure that enables anyone, anywhere to transmit and receive payments. Cryptocurrency is entirely digital, with digital transactions, entries, online purses, and online databases, as opposed to being physical money that is physically carried and traded.

This implies that advanced coding is associated with storing and transmitting digital currency information between purses and public records. Encryption's purpose is to provide security and protection.

Bitcoin, which was created in 2009 and remains the most prominent digital currency to date, was the primary digital currency in 2009. People are interested in digital currencies for their utility as a medium of exchange.

Background

In 1983, David Chaum published a paper in which he introduced the concept of virtual currency. He proposed the use of currency that could be sent untraceably without the involvement of centralized institutions. It was an automated system that made use of blind signatures for financial transactions. Later in the year 1995, Chaum invented DigiCash, a proto-cryptocurrency. This was an expansion of the encryption algorithm RSA, which was available at the time. Digicash lost popularity after Chaum declined

Microsoft Corporation's offer to acquire it, and it was discontinued in 1998.

Nick Szabo created Bit Gold in 1998, which can be considered the precursor to Bitcoin. To receive rewards, it was necessary to solve cryptographic puzzles. Bit Gold's fatal defect was that it was incapable of resolving the issue of double spending without the assistance of a central authority, which led to its demise. After the development of the Bitcoin Blockchian network in 2009 by Satoshi Nakamoto, cryptocurrency became officially recognized and utilized. Due to their reliance on a centralized network, previous currencies were unable to function correctly; therefore, a blockchain network was required to separate cryptocurrency from the influence of banks and from conventional online currency management protocols.

The formation of the bitcoin blockchain resulted in the birth of Bitcoin, one of the most prominent decentralized digital currencies. Bitcoin did not acquire popularity overnight; it took nearly a decade for it to become valuable enough for people to use it to generate wealth. Forbes is given credit for highlighting Bitcoin in their article on cryptocurrencies, which resulted in Bitcoin's prices rising from a few pennies to dollars, a significant advancement for it. The triumph of Bitcoin paved the way for the creation of numerous new currencies, such as Litecoins, PPcoin, and Name coin.

A STARTER'S GUIDE TO ICOs

Each day, the universe changes and evolves. Services such as radio and television are becoming obsolete as more and more people use the Internet. The banking and financial world is no different; just consider Bitcoin as evidence. Bitinfoshart provides a glimpse into the bitcoin network by displaying the number of wallets holding at least a modest amount of bitcoin. The figures are astronomical. All signs indicate that crypto will be the future standard of exchange.

Therefore, when terms such as ICO begin to circulate around us, we should pay attention because ICO's may not only put venture capitalists out of business and change the face of finance forever, but they also have the potential to alter how we develop as a society, as ICO's have the ability to democratize the funding of ideas better than any technology that has come before.

Others recognize Ico's Strength

Since then, many srurtosurrensie have followed in Ripple's footsteps, with Ethereum being the most prominent. The Ethereum Foundation was able to conduct one of the largest ICOs ever and continues to serve as the platform's foundation. This opened the door to an entirely new generation of initial coin offerings (many of which operate on the Ethereum network and can be found on our ICO calendar).

The ICO white paper is frequently referred to as a hybrid of a crowdfunding campaign and an IPO

(Initial Public Offering). Funding secured, the entrepreneur is permitted to launch their idea. However, the primary difference between an ICO and a crowdfunding campaign is that contributors to an ICO are not necessarily making a charitable contribution or expecting to receive something in exchange for their contribution. Instead, you are investing in the future value of the company. In this situation, they resemble a hare sold to an investor in an initial public offering.

There are, however, some fundamental differences between an ICO and an IPO. As previously stated, tokens are neither "hare" nor "euitu" within a company. However, this is where things begin to become difficult because no two tokens are created or designed to be identical. Other tokens are designed to serve as an aet's internal digital surrensu or network fuel, whereas some tokens only serve to represent the value contained within an aet. For intanse, as tokens are frequently nothing more than digital sod, they must do much more than simply signify value. The user can grant voting rights, provide an access token, and implement programmable tasks, among other capabilities.

Benefits

The Ethereum rrojest was a phenomenally successful ICO for its period (in 2014). In 2017, however, we are eeing rrojest such as Tezos raie 232 million dollar and Bansor raie 153 million dollar. The means by which these companies raise capital is phenomenal. TenX, for example, just raised approximately $80 million in seven minutes. Gnoi, an online resale market, generated approximately $12 million in ten minutes.

There are no gatekeepers in the world of Initial Coin Offerings, and this has paved the way for entrepreneurs, who may have had difficulty raising funds through more conventional VC financing, to eventually have a shot at launching their projects.

Although ICOs are breaking new ground, the product is still quite immature. The majority of initiatives are completed by reusing previous ICOs. Even the websites of many initial coin offerings (ICOs) resemble one another (e.g., futuristic moving polygon backgrounds and numerous images of network "layers").

The Possibility Of Disruption

ICOs have the ability to democratize the funding of ideas better than any previous technology.

However, ICOs are still in a very nascent stage, so we do not completely comprehend the implementation of this relatively new technology. This is one of the reasons why investors are cautioned against investing in initial coin offerings (ICOs). The ICO sonsert is still very immature; there is little supervision and little regulation. Not that this is a bad thing, as the world needs fewer gatekeepers, not more, but the emergence of new technologies has paved the way for a multitude of problems.

Potential investors consider, in addition to regulatory issues, whether the token offered will have utility outside of the project itself. Is the token backed by real value, and can investors exchange it for other assets (digital or otherwise) of value if it is only used as a "arrsoin"? The list of possible answers can be endless.

Similarly, investors are exposed to a high level of risk because the majority of ICOs operate by launching the funding round without any rrodust to show for it. In other words, individuals invest in a concept and a white paper. Often, there is nothing palpable to bask in its glory. As useful as someone may believe a project will be, the reality is that it will eventually fail. This makes funding an ICO even riskier, given the possibility that it will not achieve its objectives.

The purpose of the Ethereum ICO has been mentioned a few times, but many ICOs have failed. Some ICOs fail, causing investors to lose their entire investment, while others generate returns of over 2,000%. If you had invested $2,000 in Ethereum when it was worth $0.40 per token, you would now have $1.5 million worth of ETH.

Another issue with the public phase is the complexity of ICO participation. It is complex and non-intuitive, requiring knowledge and experience that the average user simply does not possess. To grow and truly become the next great thing, ICOs must become more accessible to the general public and user-friendly. Tehnisal restrictions impede engagement with new users who are unfamiliar with blockchain.

As previously indicated, the ICO sonsert is still in its early stages of maturity, and as the market evolves and moves in this direction, the majority of the problems addressed will eventually be eliminated. Beginning with Bitcoin, the remainder of the globe is moving toward the future of the financial world. Best wishes for the future!

Chapter 2 Successful Traders' Mental Process

Successful cryptocurrency investors think differently than novice investors.

They think that -

They can avoid cryptocurrency markets.

In cryptocurrency trading, there is no emotion.

Less-seasoned merchants engage in visceral trading.

A superior strategy will not result in greater losses.

It is not necessary for winning trades to be excellent trades.

Improving market analysis will result in significant gains.

Their mindset determines their achievement on the cryptocurrency market.

This mindset requires time and effort to develop. You cannot rush the process, and there is no sense in killing yourself when everything turns into pears.

Changing your mindset to that of a trader is difficult; it is comparable to developing muscle in a gym. Daily exertion is required to strengthen and shape the brain. You are, after all, attempting to reverse your physiology's natural response. Due to the rapid amygdala response, it may initially be challenging to implement your protocol.

Meditation can be beneficial when trading cryptocurrencies because it reduces the brain's response, allowing you to recognize emotional changes before they become overwhelming.

The best cryptocurrency speculators meditate frequently. Meditation is not 'wow wow.'

You must disregard the constant stream of thoughts that enter your consciousness and avoid becoming attached to them. Before beginning trading, a simple meditation is to close your eyes for approximately five minutes.

If you experience an emotional moment, take a step back, close your eyes, and inhale deeply. Naturally, when we close our eyelids, the brain waves slow down. Moreover, deep respiration assists in stabilizing the body's response.

Developing a Trader's Attitude

Are you up to the challenge of cultivating a brilliant mindset for trading cryptocurrencies? If so, continue.

Develop a routine of trading.

When you desire, your trading interface is excellent. However, having a daily pattern distinguishes successful crypto traders from unsuccessful ones. Start your day with some peaceful time. Eliminate distractions by leaving your cell phone in another room and turning off social media notifications.

Invest in your cryptocurrency trading education

Spend your time studying. Take courses, read books, and research the strategies of successful crypto traders.

Manage your losses

Never exceed 1% risk and always have a stop loss in place.

You will be astounded by how effective it is to record your business voyage in a daily journal.

Document each transaction

Why did you take it? What occurred afterward? Let go of your emotions of frustration in this magazine. Then, peruse it once per week and take note of your good and bad behaviors. Then, apply this knowledge to the following business week.

Get out of the way - your crypto business will succeed or fail on its own. Once you trade, you have no control. Examining your vocation activates the amygdala and compels you to work.

Timeline for Developing This Attitude

It varies from trader to trader how long it takes to cultivate a cryptocurrency-trading mindset.

The amount of time required to develop a trader's perspective depends on your dedication and self-awareness. As soon as you recognize the flaws and errors in your behaviors and emotions, you embark on the path to a trader's mindset.

The greater your daily effort, the quicker you will see results. In a few weeks or months, you can anticipate to see positive results if you persist.

Emotions Management

The cryptocurrency market is governed by emotions. Every day, thousands of retail crypto traders press the buy and sell buttons under the influence of avarice, fear, FOMO, and revenge trade.

It is difficult to diminish emotional turmoil. It requires effort, but you can initiate some helpful behaviors.

Do not gaze upon the commerce. Walk, consume a beverage, or call. Do whatever will propel you off the rankings.

Don't keep checking transactions

Ideally, you should close your charts so you can monitor the situation. This bad tendency is ideal for novice cryptocurrency traders. When the business is profitable and displaying negative figures, you will be pleased.

Three losses signifies 'Stop Trading'; tomorrow is a new day. Close the trading platform and record the results in your trading journal.

Analyze the failures; was there anything you could have done differently? Choose a trading session with minimal volatility - Cryptocurrency fluctuates at optimal times, but you should read the charts and trade when the market is stable.

Assess your feelings - How do you feel? Are you exhausted, emotional, frightened, or anxious that you might lose a profitable trade? If you feel uneasy, leave and return when your emotions are under control.

Stopping impulsive cryptocurrency trade

Identify yourself apart from results

Consider whether you are overtrading or taking more than 1% risk on your cryptocurrency transactions.

Fear and greed are the two dominant emotions of a novice cryptocurrency trader. It can be frustrating to lose a significant amount of progress. However, this perspective is a tad insane. The crypto market is enormous, with the potential for numerous daily transactions. What if a transaction is missed? Simply locate another one.

When you concentrate on the profits you have lost, you squander time searching for the next profitable trade.

Avoid being selfish. Small, additional profits are continually added to your cryptocurrency account.

Victory after defeat

Aim for the long term by gradually adding one dollar to your cryptocurrency account. Are you familiar with the tale of the tortoise and the rabbit? Yes, be a tortoise because your profits must be cultivated and safeguarded. Consider these victories to be gold particles, even if they are minor.

Professionally manage your business transactions.

Professional cryptocurrency traders do not care about the outcomes of their transactions. They diligently await a profitable trade, and when the price reaches their desired entry point, they execute the trade. Then, they abandon the enterprise. A professional crypto trader does not get excited or furious regardless of the outcome.

They are aware that a 50% success rate with 1% risk and a high RTR will always result in a profit if they maintain composure and independence.

After executing a crypto transaction, a professional trader does not micromanage it. At a certain point, the crypto trader can transfer his stop loss to Break Avon. Moreover, they do not interfere.

They may examine the trade once per day. If the price moves against the trader, he or she can end the position to avoid stop loss and wait for another entry point. Or they will trade on another cryptocurrency.

Your mindset Boost Your Profits

Yes, absolutely 100 percent.

The majority of inexperienced crypto traders believe they need a stronger strategy or trading plan. They fly from system to system for a few weeks before declaring that this strategy is ineffective.

Their mentality is something that some novice cryptocurrency traders observe. He believes he has been the victim of deception on the cryptocurrency market. They point the finger at their teachers or the literature they've read.

They never glance in the mirror and think, "Perhaps I'm to blame."

One cause for this is the 95 percent failure rate among new entrepreneurs, which can be attributed to a lack of commitment to an entrepreneurial mindset.

5 percent of effective business owners have worked on it. They were aware that their survival brain was holding them back, so they altered their approach to cryptocurrency trading.

Their beliefs and attitudes regarding cryptocurrency transactions have changed. He emphasized the psychological aspects of trading cryptocurrencies.

1% to 5% of the most successful crypto speculators meditate daily. They will not approach a crypto chart until they have prepared their minds for trading.

Invest time in developing your business mindset, and you will achieve success.

Advantages of a Trading mentality

As soon as your mind reaches this level of trading mentality, you will begin to experience unexpectedly large benefits.

The new cryptocurrency trader will no longer be quick and opportunistic. A mindset of a trader will maintain your business robust and stable.

You trade less - Professional traders assert that profitable trades do not determine their success. They do not engage in this transaction, resulting in continued expansion and increased capital.

You will enjoy trading more; the hassles of trading frequently lead to irritation and exhaustion. Attachment to a result is stressful, and when you are wounded, you cannot control your emotions.

You gain assurance - and not just regarding cryptocurrency trading. There are numerous advantages to developing a business perspective that are applicable to all aspects of your life. Your conviction in trading cryptocurrencies enables you to trade when you see favorable opportunities and avoid bad cryptocurrencies. Losing traders are crippled by the crippling self-doubt that accompanies every defeat. Even if they lose, successful traders do not bother about the doubts.

The psychology of a successful crypto speculator

The successful crypto trader has invested time refining his trading style and mentality. This mindset will not develop overnight. Numerous prosperous businessmen confess that they spent many years losing money, destroying their accounts, and shedding their hair in despair.

They did not, however, quit up.

Successful cryptocurrency speculators possess certain characteristics that contribute to their success.

They are not fearful of peril

If your risk tolerance is minimal, you will find it difficult to accept the loss. You have a 50% average victory rate and a 50% average loss rate.

Successful traders exercise self-control and situational management because they recognize that there is no assurance of success in every trade. Therefore, the initial stage in becoming a cryptocurrency trader is to develop a tolerance for risk.

They are able to adapt to market conditions

Verification bias is a significant issue for novice cryptocurrency investors. Successful crypto traders are not bound by their analysis, and they can swiftly alter their perspective on the likelihood of future price changes.

Always consider the opposite scenario when analyzing transactions to circumvent this. If you want to trade ETH, for instance, you should analyze sales transactions. This exercise affords you the opportunity to view both viewpoints of an argument without confirmation bias.

Affirmative action is the adversary in business. The brain desires to corroborate your selection. Therefore, return to the ETH trade; you can only see the purchasing opportunity and remain in the trade longer if the price moves against you.

They are constrained by discipline

They view the cryptocurrency market objectively regardless of the outcome of their open positions.

They are not enthusiastic about victory or losing

Successful crypto merchants are not elated when they win and are not disheartened when they lose. They are in control of their emotions and are not controlled by them.

5. They better manage Risk and Money

They do not engage in reckless wagering on any outcome, and they adhere to their risk percentage per transaction, which is typically 1%. Before entering a crypto transaction, a successful trader weighs the risk against the potential reward.

Successful traders believe that a winning trade may not be a good trade and that a losing trade may not be a poor trade.

It is your task if you run out of money but have done everything correctly in your trade. The truth is that it has been lost. A profitable enterprise is one that offers a larger return than risk.

Successful cryptocurrency merchants consider possibilities and only engage in transactions with a high probability of success. Anything short of this perspective is wagering. A lucrative transaction that ends in victory is undesirable.

This mentality is the primary distinction between losing and successful crypto traders.

Variety Of Cryptocurrencies

Since the introduction of bitcoin, hundreds of new cryptocurrencies have entered the market. Following the triumph of Bitcoin, numerous alternative cryptocurrencies, or altcoins, have been introduced, and their number has increased to 700. Some are sold for less than Bitcoin, while others are typically more accessible. This section of the book describes the twelve most prominent cryptocurrencies. Perhaps you are already familiar with Bitcoin and have some questions about how it operates, but this time you will enter the realm of cryptocurrencies and learn what the playful currencies are.

1. the Bitcoin

Bitcoin is the first and most prominent cryptocurrency in the world; however, its existence as a global payment system is unknown to some. Bitcoin is founded on mathematical proofs rather than a bank. Similar to E-mail technology, no one owns or controls the Bitcoin system. Even the group and individual behind it remain unknown; only the pseudonym Satoshi Nakamoto has been made public.

To have Bitcoin on hand, you must first create an online wallet. Yes, you can sign up for a variety of online wallets for virtual currency, and all of them are free to use. You can also use digital currency exchangers such as Coinbase, Kraken, Bitstamp, CEX.IO, and BitFinex. The next step is to acquire bitcoins directly from other people using online marketplaces. The majority of exchangers require you to link your cards or bank accounts in order to make a purchase. You can now navigate to the buy section of the exchange and select the quantity of bitcoin you wish to purchase. Bitcoin's value fluctuates over time; it can increase or decrease – nobody knows. The 'Blockchain' public ledger functions as a record of each Bitcoin transaction.

The blockchain consists of a growing collection of records known as blocks that are protected by cryptography; once a block has been recorded, it cannot be altered.

Bitcoin can be used for purchasing commodities, sending money, booking travel online, and purchasing digital products; this eliminates the need for middlemen, i.e., banks.

2. Ethereum

In 2011, a Toronto-based programmer named Vitalik Buterin became initially interested in Bitcoin. Buterin, who was 19 years old at the time, founded Bitcoin Magazine and wrote hundreds of articles about the cryptocurrency world. In 2013, Buterin has published the white paper. Describes an alternative platform designed for any decentralized application a developer may wish to create. The system was subsequently named Ethereum, and, like Bitcoin, it is a decentralized public blockchain network. However, there are some technical differences between the two cryptocurrencies, as miners in Ethereum labor to earn Ether rather than Bitcoin. Ether is a piece of code that enables a program or application to run; no one possesses Ether, but the system that supports its functionality costs money. Ether, unlike Bitcoin, has no maximum supply; 13 million Ether are mined annually.

To acquire Ether, you must locate someone online or in person who has it and is willing to trade it for cash. If you want to have Ether on hand, you also have the option of purchasing Bitcoin from reputable exchanges and then exchanging it for Ether.

3. Litecoin

This cryptocurrency is also generated by mining; it was established in October 2011 by the former Google engineer Charles Lee. Litecoin is designed to reduce the time required to mine a block from ten minutes to two and a half minutes. Because it employs the "scrypt algorithm," which favors a large amount of high-speed RAM, the aforementioned digital currency has faster transactions than bitcoin. This is why scrypt is known as the "memory hard problem." Similar to Bitcoin, Litecoin has a maximum supply of 84 million coins and a market capitalization of $540,274,528.26.

Litecoin can manage a high transaction volume Reduces double-spending attacks Fast confirmation for merchants in particular

4. Swell

What is Wave? IsRipplesameasBitcoin? Well,it'sa huge NO.Ripple is a network for currency exchange and remittances that employs a network-managed common ledger and is validated by independent servers. Formerly known as OpenCoin, Ripple Labs was founded by CEO Chris Larsen and CTO Jed McCaleb, both of whom have extensive knowledge of digital currency. Jed McCaleb is presently responsible for the majority of Bitcoin transactions worldwide. While Larsen was a co-founder of the financial company E-LOAN, the remainder of the Ripple developers have experience with Bitcoin. Ripple is based on a shared public database, which is a stark contrast to Bitcoin, which is generated through energy- and computing-intensive proof of work. Ripple does not use blockchain technology; the company's objective is to maintain the free passage of funds.

5. Dash

Dash was initially introduced as Xcoin, then altered its name to Darkcoin, and in 2015 it was rebranded as Dash, which is now the sixth largest cryptocurrency. Dash is a peer-to-peer cryptocurrency that was forked from Bitcoin in order to make transactions quicker and more private. Dash is the first cryptocurrency to have a decentralized blockchain governance system, similar to many other cryptocurrencies. Dash is also attempting to address some of Bitcoin's shortcomings. It offers its consumers faster transactions and increased anonymity. Dash transactions are completed in four seconds, whereas Bitcoin transactions typically take ten minutes to complete. Dash is also mined in the same manner as Bitcoin.

6. Monero

Monero is the most anonymous cryptocurrency when it comes to transaction privacy. It is a secure and untraceable currency system that employs a special form of cryptography to ensure that all transactions are completely untraceable. After its debut in 2014, the Monero has attained a high level of popularity due to its privacy-oriented characteristics. The Monero mining procedure is founded on the egalitarian principle.

7. IOTA

IOTA is unlike the vast majority of online currencies in that it is designed for machines but cannot be mined. IOTA is an acronym for 'Internet of Things

Application'; it solves the scalability problems of blockchain and transaction fees simultaneously by eliminating the block and chain. To transmit a transaction to the IOTA ledger, it is merely necessary to verify two prior transactions. The entire supply of coins is capped at 2,779,530,283,271,761 units. This cryptocurrency does not require miners to power up the network, and there is no central ledger.

8. Zcash

Roger Ver, Barry Seibert, and Pantera Capital launched Zcashis on October 28, 2016. Zcash is a decentralized and open-source cryptocurrency that employs a secure network dubbed zk-snark. This unique feature enables the network to maintain and secure the ledger without disclosing the transaction quantities.

9. Stellar

Jed McCaleb, co-founder of Ripple, is also the creator of Stellar, a cryptocurrency and payment technology. Stellar is comparable to other payment technologies in that a decentralized server manages the network with a distributed ledger that is updated every two to five seconds. It employs Federated Byzantine Agreement (FBA) Algorithm, which facilitates faster transactions, as opposed to relying solely on miners.

10. NEM

NEM is introduced on 31 March 2015 as a peer-to-peer cryptocurrency and blockchain platform written in Java and C++. NEM, which stands for "New Economy Movement," has its own consensus algorithm, unlike most other cryptocurrencies. This can prevent assaults on the network and on all transactions. NEM intends to develop a smart asset blockchain capable of handling high workloads.

11. NEO

Da Hongfei founded NEO, the first decentralized and open-source cryptocurrency in China. Neo is both a cryptocurrency and blockchain platform; it was established in 2014 as 'Antshares' and rebranded as 'NEO' in June 2017. Using the Byzantine Fault-Tolerance (Dbft) consensus mechanism, Neo can sustain 10,000 transactions per second.

This cryptocurrency was introduced on September 9, 2017 and was created by the Singapore-based TRON Foundation, a non-profit organization. Tron is a decentralized, open-source cryptocurrency with an application feature. The technology of Tron is a storage facility that enables users to access content in every region of the globe, independent of the Google Play Store. It also enables content creators to profit from content sharing.

13. Steem

Steem is a blockchain-based platform for social media where users can receive rewards. Steemit was introduced in July 2016 and presently has 70,000 users; since then, it has grown substantially.

Steem is very distinct from other cryptocurrencies because it has a built-in inflation rate of 100% per year and no coin limit. Steem supports online communities and even social media platforms by offering virtual currency as compensation.

The Growth Of Additional Cryptocurrencies

Altcoins or alternative cryptocurrencies proliferated as Bitcoin garnered popularity and mainstream attention. These alternative cryptocurrencies were established with the intention of enhancing or expanding the original concept of Bitcoin. Others sought to resolve perceived Bitcoin network weaknesses, such as scalability and energy efficiency.

The concept of a decentralized application, or DApp, is central to the design of a number of altcoins. A DApp is a software application that operates on a decentralized network, indicating that it is not under the control of a single entity. DApps have the potential to disrupt numerous industries, including finance, healthcare, supply chain management, and voting systems.

In addition to altcoins and decentralized applications (DApps), initial coin offerings (ICOs) also emerged alongside the rise of cryptocurrencies. In an initial coin offering, a company or initiative issues a new cryptocurrency in exchange for funds. ICOs have become a popular method for entrepreneurs and other organizations to raise capital, but they have also been subject to significant scrutiny and regulation due to fears of fraud and a lack of transparency.

The proliferation of altcoins and the emergence of initial coin offerings have added a new level of complexity and diversity to the industry as the cryptocurrency landscape continues to evolve and expand. In the following chapter, we will investigate the increasing acceptance of cryptocurrency by merchants and consumers, as well as the emergence of user-friendly cryptocurrency exchanges and wallets.

The Adoption Of Cryptocurrency By The Masses

As the cryptocurrency ecosystem has matured, mainstream acceptance and adoption have increased. Increasing numbers of merchants and consumers accept cryptocurrency as payment, and a growing number of financial institutions and payment processors are integrating cryptocurrency into their systems.

The development of cryptocurrency exchanges, which enable users to buy, sell, and trade a variety of cryptocurrencies, has been one of the primary drivers of mainstream adoption. These exchanges have made it simpler for people to access and utilize cryptocurrency, and have also contributed to market liquidity and stability.

In addition to exchanges, the development of wallets that are more user-friendly has contributed to the widespread adoption of cryptocurrencies. A wallet is a software application that stores and manages a user's cryptocurrency. Wallets were often difficult to use and required a high level of technical expertise in the early days of Bitcoin. However, the development of more user-friendly wallets has made it simpler for individuals to begin using cryptocurrency and contributed to its increased popularity among a broader audience.

Stablecoins and other instruments that bridge the divide between the traditional financial system and the decentralized world of cryptocurrency are another factor that has contributed to the widespread adoption of cryptocurrencies. Stablecoins are cryptocurrencies pegged to a stable asset, such as the U.S. dollar, and designed to reduce price volatility. By utilizing stablecoins and other instruments, it is possible to use cryptocurrency within the traditional financial system in a more seamless and integrated manner.

In the following chapter, we will examine the legal and regulatory challenges confronting the cryptocurrency industry, as well as the tension between cryptocurrency's decentralized nature and the desire for oversight and control.

From this point forward until the end of the chapter, everything is BTC-specific.

In the middle of 2010, the hash rate (the number of hashes calculated per second across the Bitcoin network) was 1 billion per second. What does this entail? In other words, regardless of the number of individuals or the speed of their computers and processors, collectively they attempted 1 billion hashes per second to generate the block's desired hash. This is the format with the thirty zeros in front, or something similar. Bitcoin controlled this format; if it desired, it could request 10 zeros. I'll go into greater detail in the following section.

The year was 2010.

The universal hash rate was 22 million Terahashes per second last week, at the time of composing this book in 2018 (last week). This corresponds to 22 trillion trillion hashes per second. This is a staggering amount of processing capacity! It indicates that Bitcoin mining activity is extremely high. However, this also implies that in order for Bitcoin to maintain a ten-minute interval between the release of new coins, it must increase the difficulty of the conundrum.

Remember that we just discussed this. Instead of increasing the rate at which it floods the market with coins, the algorithm demands a puzzle with a reduced probability of success when the computing power is so great. Therefore, it requires a harder-to-obtain proof of work, and you must ultimately perform more computations to obtain more hashes. In the end, the difficulty is increased to such a degree that the interval between reward events returns to ten minutes.

Currently, the computing capacity is approximately 22 billion quadrillion hashes per second. This means that per minute, 1,320 billion trillion hashes are being calculated around the globe, contributing this amount of computing power to generate this amount of work.

Here is how the calculation is performed. The typical hash rate is available on the Bitcoin website. The hash rate is shared by all miners in the network, although the exact number of miners is unknown. We are aware that there are very few individual miners remaining. Currently, the majority of them are either professionally managed or combined into sizable groups.

This is why.

With 22 million trillion hashes per second, 1.32×10^{25} hashes must be solved prior to obtaining the correct nonce and receiving the block reward. The reason we know this is because Bitcoin has a ten-minute production rate. That is, if you aggregate the quantity of computing power, you will need no more than that amount of computing power to reach the solution.

Here, a definite conclusion can be drawn. First, if you are only using your home or office PC, don't bother. It is impossible for this to operate.

Second, you must increase your hash rate as much as feasible to achieve periodic wins. Let's suppose there are only two people in the world who can negotiate solutions. In the long run, the logic dictates that the two will have equal chances and outcomes. Both will achieve 50 percent of the outcome. The percentage of chance, however, is determined by comparing the total computing capacity. In actuality, this is how it operates. Your probability of striking the block is proportional to the ratio of your hash rate to the total hash rate of the universe.

A few factors contribute to increased profits in the mining industry. The first is that your hashing rate is higher. Antminer S9 has the greatest hash rate currently available for purchase; it costs approximately $2,000 and generates 12.9 Terahashes per second. If you operate your machines properly and provide them with adequate cooling, they will last at least three years.

Let's say you have a complete understanding of your fixed costs if you know they will last approximately three years and will cost you $2,000; for example, if you know they will cost

$2000. The next factor to consider is the price of your electricity.

From there, you can input the information into a calculator to determine how much you can earn per month. There are a number of excellent and potent profitability calculators that you can use to determine if you can consistently generate a profit using the miner of your choosing. You are not required to acquire an Antminer, but you must acquire a device that can consistently generate a high hash rate.

Regarding the qualitative and quantitative aspects of deciding to begin mining, there are a number of considerations to bear in mind. First, you must determine your budget for investing in hardware. After that, you should consider what equipment will be required. Suppose, for example, I have $20,000 to invest in a Bitcoin mining operation. This will allow me to purchase approximately nine Antminer S9 miners, with the remainder going towards rack, fans, and cables. Then, you will need a location to store the equipment. If you only have nine miners, a basic rack in your room will suffice; however, you must ensure that your room has sufficient airflow and cooling capacity. If you do not maintain proper cooling, you will likely destroy your equipment, which can rapidly become very costly.

Then, examine your monthly electric receipt to determine how much your utility charges per kilowatt-hour. This information is necessary because mining is an energy-intensive endeavor.

Once you have gathered this information, use an online mining calculator to examine your monthly profit projections. Currently, what information does the calculator require from you?

The initial requirement is the difficulty rating. You can find the current Bitcoin difficulty rate by visiting Google and inputting "current Bitcoin difficulty rate." I just verified for this example and the current difficulty level is 1,590,896,927,258. You must enter this number into the calculator.

Inputting this into the calculator will require you to determine the hash rate of your miner. If you only have one miner, then use that miner's hash rate. In this example, however, you have nine, so if your hash rate for one Antminer is 12.9 TH/s, it will be 116.1 TH/s for nine. Just plug it in.

Additionally, the power rating of your mining equipment will be required. Check its power rating and multiply it by the number of devices you're operating. My sample miner consumes 1,375 watts per miner in this instance. Given that I have nine, that is 12,375 Watts. You must also determine the cost of utilities. Here in California, mine costs 12 cents.

Lastly, you must input the expense of the equipment. After entering this information, I must also enter the exchange rate between BTC and USD. Currently, one Bitcoin costs just north of

$8,000 USD. Using the calculator, I determine that I will earn 0.535 BTC per month based on the inputs given. In addition, my electric bill will exceed $1,000. In that month, I will earn slightly more than $3,400.

Therefore, if I earn $3,400, I will break even in six months, assuming the BTC/USD exchange rate remains constant. After six months, I begin to generate a profit. At the current exchange rate, my annual profit would be 100% in the first year, 200% in the second, and again 200% in the third. This assumes there is no increase in electricity costs, mining difficulty, or the number of miners over the next three years.

Obviously, we cannot be certain about any of that. However, there are some general guidelines you should observe.

The first is that if the exchange rate rises, the number of individuals entering the mine will increase, and so will the difficulty. If you wish to maintain the same ratios, you must increase your own investment proportionally; however, this is not always feasible in these circumstances. You possess two options. You can save money on utilities by relocating the operations to a state where the cost of living is lower. In the previous example, I used twelve cents. If that was cut in half, my profit would increase to $3,960.

The second alternative is that the cost of the apparatus has a substantial effect on the investment. The best method to evaluate it is by comparing the hash rate to the price. Therefore, the Antminer S9, which costs $2,000 and has a hash rate of 12 TH/s, provides me with 6 billion hashes per second per dollar. If you divide all of your options by the number of hashes per second per dollar, you will have a clearer picture.

That's one approach, but there's an even superior one, particularly if you can compare their profitability based on wattage. Then, divide the final result by the total wattage of your mining equipment: 6 billion hashes per second per dollar divided by the total wattage of your mining rig. In my case, this number was 1375, so my final result would be: 4,363,636 hashes per second per dollar per watt.

This number has no significance in isolation. However, in order for this to make sense, it must be compared to other systems and configurations. Suppose you examine the Antminer R4. In this instance, the R4 costs roughly $1000, or half the price. Again, I'll invest $20,000, so let's compare apples to apples to determine how much I earn.

Using the same inputs, I invest $20,000, spend $18,000 on hardware to purchase 18 individual parts, and retain $2,000 for incidental costs. I am left with an 18-person mining equipment, and according to the calculator, I earn $4,800 per month. This is a marginally higher profit rate than the previous one I had with the S9, as I only made approximately $3,400. That is a substantial difference in terms of profit potential.

It can also be viewed in the second manner I mentioned, with 8 billion hashes per second per dollar. This number is obtained by dividing the hash rate by the price, minus 8.6 TH/s by 1,000 dollars. This results in 8.6 billion TH/s per dollar. Afterwards, divide this amount by 845 watts. This corresponds to 10,177,514 hashes per second per dollar and watt.

In this case, the R4 is the uncontested winner. It has a larger hashing capacity than the S9 when stacked multiple times. The S9 is simple to use if you only intend to operate one.

Mining Technique

When you commence Bitcoin mining, you can choose from a variety of mining strategies. Complete entry is the first order of business. Do not invest less than $2,000 or $3,000 to try the waters in this market. That is a waste of time and effort. You will lose money and develop a disdain for the industry and yourself as a result of your failure. That money would be better spent taking the males out for a beer.

When playing this game, keep in mind the adage that "there is strength in numbers." Set up the system in the building's coldest room with the help of a couple of companions and a minimum of $100,000.

The majority of individuals are unaware that preventing processes from overheating depends not only on the number of fans, but also on sustaining their optimal temperature. Overheating is a major concern, but optimal temperatures increase the average hash rate.

In the winter, if necessary, open the windows; in the summer, turn up the air conditioning and direct the blowers out of the room. If you have an attic fan, you can regulate the ventilation in your home or workplace effectively.

Next, you must invest in backup ventilation and generators. The generators are not designed to keep processors operating if the power goes out. They exist to keep the fans operating in the event of a power outage. If you do not run the fans and the processors abruptly stop, they are still generating heat, and now the fans are off as well. This is a problem. Therefore, ensure that you have a backup power source to operate the fans and to gently shut them down after a power outage.

Use the equipment nonstop. Running equipment at reduced intervals does not increase its longevity; keeping it cool does.

You will now access the game. This company is comparable to all others. The time for viewing bitcoin mining as a diversion or pastime has long since passed. Bitcoin mining is a serious business that requires an understanding of cryptocurrencies, the fundamentals of cryptography as they relate to coins, and the operating systems and software required to get this hardware to run at the most efficient rate possible. There are a variety of adjustments and add-ons you can use to maximize the performance of your rig.

Choosing to Mine for Bitcoin

At the conclusion of the day, you must concentrate on two queries. Are you interested in cryptocurrency mining? You should not erroneously believe that you can mine cryptocurrencies without prior consideration and preparation. In the end, it is just like any other business, requiring an investment, the potential for risk and profit, and consistent effort and problem solving. Not to mention the need for constant talent development. It does not imply that anyone who can turn on a computer can earn money mining. Even if you join a group, you must have some knowledge of what you are doing in order to overcome any obstacles along the path.

After deciding to mine coins, for a variety of reasons, you must realize that everything reduces down to a single factor.

Let me clarify.

There are a number of factors that go into evaluating the infrastructure and mining capacity, as evidenced by a web search. Yes, these tasks are necessary when deciding which miner to purchase. However, these are not the same considerations you must make when choosing which coin to invest in. There are minor adjustments that work best if you are an expert in one field. The learning curve may not be precipitous, but it does exist, and as time passes, it will be far more advantageous for you to be an expert at one thing than at several.

Aside from hardware and energy costs, as well as time devoted to the project and startup costs, there is only one item you must study and comprehend. That is the current Bitcoin market price. Why? Because unless you reside in an area where bitcoin has permeated every aspect of life, you will still have to convert your bitcoin to legal tender in order to buy groceries, get your hair cut, pay for gas, utilities, cable, and even your child's lunch. You know, into dollars or whatever currency you use.

Consequently, you will need to keep a watch on the exchange rate. Consider it this way. If you purchased a piece of land that is rumored to contain gold deposits, you must determine the market price of gold. If you believe that the price of gold will continue to rise, then you are aware that future profits will make the investment beneficial.

This is the most important factor: where you believe the price of bitcoin will be in the short and long term.

This is a question you must address yourself. It is the matter of strategy. Regardless of how hard you work, if the price of bitcoin remains stagnant or depreciates, you will find it less appealing. This is a decision you must make immediately. There is no correct response, but once you make a choice, you must live with it.

Additionally, you must choose which currency you will use, as the hardware, settings, and learning curve are distinct for each. As I've previously stated, you should be an authority in the one you select, and this expertise comes from experience.

List Of Suggested Cryptocurrency Ventures For Profitable Investment

This is one of the likely currencies with significant potential for 2023. During the presale period, it has already generated over 80% of sales, raising over $4 million. This accomplishment is unprecedented in the world of cryptocurrencies, prompting experts to predict that it will soon be listed on major trading platforms.

Dash 2 Trade is underpinned by the ERC-20 standard of the Ethereum blockchain. This is the most inclusive and secure standard, which will increase your confidence in your coin. Additionally, it ensures that the token is effectively and efficiently exchanged.

Token owners have access to the Dash 2 Trade platform, where trustworthy information is traded based on membership status. Free memberships provide access to basic on-chain data, while paid memberships provide access to crypto analytics, insights, and metrics.

The D2T token was co-created by professionals who are enthusiastic about providing traders with access to all market research so they can incorporate it into effective trading strategies. As a result, the D2T has become one of the year's finest investments and will continue to be significant.

Shiba Inu (SHIB)

Similar to Dogecoin, this is a meme coin. Since its 2020 release, its popularity has been difficult to contest. Its developers are diligently working to add more features so that it has practical applications, which could increase its popularity.

The entry into the metaverse will be facilitated by Shiberse, one of their most recent ventures. According to the most recent information, consumers will be able to purchase up to 100,600 Shiberse land parcels. Within the Shiberse, users are able to create and administer projects in districts such as Breeds, Currency, Growth, and Technology.

Shiba Inu is an additional investment opportunity before its popularity rises again.

Apecoin (APE) is a cryptocurrency.

Apecoin is a platform that employs 10,000 distinct, non-fungible, collectible Bored Ape tokens (NFTs). On this market, some of the most valuable non-fungible tokens are founded on the Ethereum blockchain. The Bored Ape Yacht Club was unveiled by its creators in 2022.

The greatest feature is that Apecoin users receive a 2% discount when making online purchases with the token.

ApeCoin is an ERC-20 token based on Ethereum with governance and utility functions. It was designed as a Metaverse-specific cryptocurrency. It can be used to make online purchases with Shopping.io. Users now have access to products from retailers including Walmart, Amazon, Home Depot, eBay, and others. Coinbase, a cryptocurrency exchange, handles all transactions.

IMPT.io

IMPT.io (IMPT) is another cryptocurrency that has the potential to take the world by storm. It is regarded as one of the best "green" coins, or coins that combine technology and sustainability.

The IMPT marketplace is then utilized to collect the consumer credits. In addition, users have the option to utilize their preferred mint for NFTs.

In addition to reducing the greenhouse effect, IMPT is one of the green currencies with the potential for a 50x increase.

By providing users with carbon credits, which they obtain by conducting business with particular companies, the founders and developers ensure that users reduce their carbon footprint. Over ten thousand of these brands are environmentally conscious and support the environmental movement.

Investors who desire to participate can connect their Trust or Metamask wallets during the presale phase of the currency. Since investors are informed of the gas fee in advance, the process is transparent and devoid of covert fees.

Calvaria (RIA)

The coin gas has been attracting the interest of cryptocurrency investors due to its promising future. With its Play-to-Earn feature, it is lowering the barrier between crypto technology and non-crypto individuals.

This application allows players to acquire bitcoin without a wallet. More participants means more winnings for the victors.

It is optional for players to purchase in-game items such as crypto tokens, NFTs, and other items. As a result, gamers will find it more acceptable. Anyone with a functional mobile device can access their currency from anywhere.

You can capitalize on the fact that RIA is currently in its presale period by purchasing and holding the stock.

Tamadoge (TAMA)

The next coin is Tamadoge, which was one of the most anticipated cryptocurrency initiatives of 2022 prior to its release. It is a meme coin, similar to Dogecoin, but also stands out for other reasons that enhance its potential.

Tamadoge's Tamaverse will house multiple initiatives and enable investors to diversify their holdings. In addition, this metaverse includes a feature known as "play to earn" that enables players to play and collect cryptocurrency tokens. Tamaverse allows users to create a virtual pet, educate it, and compete against other pets. Through their actions and victories, they can acquire Dogecoin, which can be converted into Tamadogecoins.

On Opensea, its NFT initiative was ranked among the top five NFT projects. With the addition of Augmented Reality and additional NFTs, it is anticipated that Tamadoge will win the affections of many people in 2023. On its current listings on OKX and Lbank, investors can buy and sell other cryptocurrencies with it.

An Ecosystem for Luxury Investment Properties, The Hideaways Founded on NFT

The Hideaways is a cryptocurrency worth investigating for investors seeking a currency with real-world utility that promises to transform the real estate market. This is the world's first luxury real estate investment platform, allowing consumers to invest as little as $100 in a professionally managed portfolio of luxury homes. In addition, it has the potential to expand by 20 to 50 times while maintaining a reasonable market capitalization.

The portfolio of luxurious properties owned by The Hideaways has a connection to each NFT. Consequently, the minimal value of the NFT is always correlated with the market price of the underlying physical asset. The NFT is then divided into tiny parts, allowing investors to purchase shares for as little as $100 in advance.

The Hideaways ecosystem provides users with the following benefits:

The property's appreciation in value

primary market NFT earnings

Passive earnings from rental properties

HDWY Staking pays off

By holding NFTs, investors can profit from both the capital appreciation of the luxury property and the exposure to the secondary NFT market. In addition, all luxury homes generate rental income for their proprietors.

Each property is acquired using a special-purpose vehicle, a legal entity with a bank account to collect rental income. After all expenses have been paid, the rental profit is distributed to NFT holders at the end of each month.

MetaBlaze

GameFi is one of the most rapidly expanding cryptocurrency industries. This new blockchain gaming industry has a great deal of expansion potential. MetaBlaze desires to modify the playing field.

MetaBlaze, a Web3 gaming startup, is reimagining the play-to-earn environment and creating a more immersive gaming experience.

By providing a Certik KYC Gold certification, a Smart Contract Audit, and Skynet monitoring, the company provides complete Web 3 transparency.

Built on the Binance Smart Chain, the MetaBlaze Token (MBLZ) is the ecosystem's native cryptocurrency. With the introduction of the first rotating rewards pool in the world, MetaBlaze's users can now participate to win Bitcoin, Ethereum, BNB, Solana, and other popular cryptocurrencies.

MetaBlaze is adopting a realistic strategy to attract players, immerse them in the story, and introduce them to the MetaBlaze gaming universe by publishing a number of small NFT games. During the development of the AAA RPG, which will include all gameplay and story elements from previous iterations.

Bitcoin MetaBlaze

The MetaBlaze team has ambitious plans for Web 3 social media integration. A recent Ask Me Anything (AMA) with the MetaBlaze team discussed the development of a Web 3-integrated social media platform for gamers and social media creators that would be available on the iTunes and Google Play stores, but no official announcement has been made as of yet. Undoubtedly, the official announcement and publication will have a substantial effect on the value of the $MBLZ coin.

The MetaBlaze ICO is already in its final phase, and it is only a matter of time before the $4 million hard cap is reached. This is your final opportunity to participate and receive a 5% MBLZ incentive.

Investors can join the MetaBlaze Telegram channel, which has over 15,000 members, to obtain the most recent information and engage in direct conversations with the team.

Battle Infinity (IBAT) is an additional candidate for the best cryptocurrency currently available. Battle Infinity is a metaverse-based play-to-earn (P2E) ecosystem that has undertaken KYC verification by CoinSniper. In this metaverse, users can create their own avatars and compete in Battle Infinity's contests to win large prizes.

Battle Infinity, whose presale was one of the quickest to sell out this year, is in development and aims to increase the popularity of metaverse-based platforms. Six distinct platforms are available to players within the Battle Infinity ecosystem. A notable example is the IBAT Premier League, which provides a blockchain-based fantasy sports league with non-fungible tokens.

In addition, Battle Infinity has an integrated NFT marketplace where users can purchase and sell their own products to customize their avatars and mint and sell their own artwork. Battle Infinity users will also be able to purchase virtual land parcels for use with in-game billboard advertising. Battle Infinity's ecosystem will also include a DeFi exchange (IBAT Battle Swap) that facilitates seamless token transferring.

Battle Infinity's ecosystem will be powered by the world's native $IBAT BEP-20 currency. The supply of 10 billion $IBAT tokens will be used for rewards distribution and staking. During the presale, investors were able to acquire 28% of the total supply.

Overall, $IBAT appears to have a good chance of becoming one of the year's top metaverse currencies, as the platform's engaging fantasy league component encourages skillful participation. The NFT structure of the fantasy league players provides a novel approach to trading and planning while constructing a team.

The best method to track the project's development and release schedule is through the Battle Infinity Telegram channel; however, moderators will never direct message you first.

The Battle Infinity (IBAT) coin was advertised on PancakeSwap following an extremely successful presale. IBAT soared 700% from its pre-sale price on the first day of trading to reach a market value of $60 million, and then surged again after being listed on LBank in late August.

IBAT Price

The coin has a current market value of $22.6 million, which is entirely diluted, but it is still a bargain given that additional listings and staking are planned for the near future. In order to collect incentives, token holders will be able to store up their tokens for 30, 60, 90, or 360 days, although the APY has not yet been disclosed.

Lucky BLOCK

Lucky Block, a recently created cryptocurrency, debuted its eagerly anticipated first prize draw and NFT prize draw in late May 2022.

Lucky Block, a platform for NFT contests, aims to revolutionize the NFT industry by offering exciting reward opportunities. Lucky Block intends to achieve success by leveraging the power of "Web 3.0" decentralized networks to liberate the world from the control of centralized operators.

On the Lucky Block platform, users can purchase NFTs for a chance to receive prizes in the corresponding category. These incentives surpass those offered by other major websites and include gaming consoles, extravagant vacations, a Bored Ape Yacht Club (BAYC) NFT, and even $1 million in Bitcoin.

The objective of Lucky Block is to completely replace, or at the very least supplement, the services offered by the current market leaders with an inclusive, truly global system. Everything is, so to say, up for grabs. Lucky Block is the finest cryptocurrency under $1.

Lucky Block recently upgraded its second ERC-20 token to version 2, allowing it to be listed on additional cryptocurrency exchanges. In contrast to the 12% trading expenses of the V1 token, this enables tax-free transactions.

Through the token bridge, holders of V1 tokens can simply upgrade to V2.

The V2 token was listed on MEXC and Gate.io in August, and additional listings are anticipated. In order to reduce the supply of tokens and increase their value, the project has also announced a 1% monthly burn.

Decentralized Mana (MANA)

Decentraland is another cryptocurrency initiative with a unique perspective that focuses on the metaverse. Users have numerous opportunities to acquire tokens through this game's platform.

In Decentraland, users are able to purchase virtual plots with either local or metaverse currency. Users can purchase in-game items and NFTs from the platform's NFT store. In addition, it provides a play-to-earn feature that allows users to passively earn money.

Decentraland, one of the most important initiatives in the metaverse, will be profitable to invest in in 2022 and take off in 2023.

FightOut

FightOut is the finest cryptocurrency for the long term due to its real-world gyms and M2E fitness app.

FightOut is our top overall long-term cryptocurrency investment due to its aspirations to create Web3-integrated gyms all over the globe, as well as the fact that it is a recently announced presale project with significant funding.

With tokens costing only $0.016, the presale has already raised more than $2 million in less than five days since its debut.

Despite substantial investment in move-to-earn initiatives in 2021 and 2022, the technology has not yet reached its full potential, with a small user base deterred by high initial costs for NFTs and lackluster compensation programs.

FightOut will avoid both of these pitfalls by allowing users to access their customized app for a small fee and by providing a reliable reward system that allows players to redeem discounts, personal training sessions, apparel, fitness gear, and supplements using in-app currency REPS.

FightOut, which claims to be one of the best cryptocurrencies to purchase right now, provides users with a customized workout program. To construct a comprehensive digital profile, smart technology is used to measure movement and key effort indicators, as well as to account for sleep patterns and nutrition.

Maximum FGHT token supply is 10 billion coins, of which 60% will be used for the presale and the remaining 30% for the rewards pool and project expansion.

RobotEra

Despite the fact that RobotEra's presale just began in November 2022, the game's incentive system and multiple in-game methods to monetize assets make it an excellent long-term investment.

Since investors can profit from GameFi ventures regardless of market direction, they have proven to be more bear-resistant than other assets in this market.

This play-to-earn project combines gaming, NFT ownership, and metaverse land ownership in order to provide a diverse ecosystem with multiple earning opportunities in what is widely regarded as one of the best crypto games available.

Following a catastrophic event, players of the LBank Labs project RobotEra must use robot NFT avatars to reconstruct the planet Taro.

In addition to mining minerals, cultivating holy trees, and using in-game tools to construct robot companions, players can use TARO tokens to purchase metaverse parcels of land and restore the planet.

As with any structures constructed on the land parcels, the NFT robots can be entirely upgraded, customized, and eventually sold as separate NFTs.

In RobotEra, players can submit original NFT works to be exhibited in museums, link to other worlds, participate in concerts, and host events, which allows for additional incentives.

Players are rewarded for possessing distinct continents, and tokens can be staked for passive income as an additional method of globe construction.

Players can fully develop metaverse land by constructing buildings and infrastructure, earning money by renting billboard space to real advertisers, and charging admission to events.

Using the game's proprietary tools and the ability to include physics, sound, user interaction, payment options, and dynamic 3D landscapes, players can create their own metaverse lands without prior coding knowledge.

With few restrictions on what can be created and added to the metaverse plots, the game's designers anticipate that new use cases will emerge gradually.

Investors can peruse the RobotEra whitepaper for project details or subscribe to the Telegram channel to track its development.

The developers of the project have been doxxed and KYC-verified, and the token smart contract has been examined by SharkTeam.

Various Crypto Currencies And Choosing The Best

Daily, new cryptocurrencies are introduced to the market. At the time of writing, there are well over a thousand, and it is unknown where the number will halt.

Many have been constructed solely to ride the bandwagon and will never be valuable. Many will vanish swiftly. But a select few, those utilizing the finest blockchain technology and backed by real value and a strong team, will survive and likely continue to expand. However, it is important to remember that this is a highly volatile market where large gains and losses occur frequently.

With so many new cryptocurrencies entering the market, it is difficult to determine which ones represent the greatest investment opportunity.

No one knows precisely how the market will behave in the future, so I cannot predict which cryptocurrencies will be the best investments. However, this is current information about the major participants.

Bitcoin: Traded under the symbol (BTC). This was the first cryptocurrency ever created. Unknown person with the alias Satoshi Nakomoto developed the concept for Bitcoin. Prior to their 2009 introduction, Nakomoto mined over one million coins at a cost of $0.008 per coin. Since then, their value has increased, making them the most valuable coin in the globe. They employ the original blockchain technology and encryption security measures.

Ethereum: Symbolized by (ETH). A digital currency with a rapid growth rate and massive benefits in 2017. It was conceived by the Russian-born programmer and cryptocurrency researcher Vatalik Buterin. Before the launch on June 30, 2015, the pre-mining of 11,9 million "ether" coins was completed.

Litecoin is traded under the symbol (LTC). On October 13, 2011, services conceived by Charlie Lee, a former Google employee, went live. It utilizes the same blockchain technology as Bitcoin, but has a quicker trading period.

Traded Ripple (XRP). Ryan Fugger first conceived of the idea in 2004. On October 6, 2015, it was renamed Ripple from its original identity, Opencoin. Then, in September 2016, Ripple announced that a number of institutions, including The Royal Bank of Canada, Bank of America, Union Credit, Santander, Westpac Banking Corporation, and Standard Chartered, were interested in joining their newly formed Global Payments Steering Group GPSG. Today, their Ripple protocol is utilized by numerous international institutions and American Express.

When deciding which cryptocurrency to invest in, it is essential to conduct extensive research. It is a highly volatile market where significant gains and losses are possible.

When searching for a coin that has the potential to appreciate substantially in value, it is not enough to consider the coin's price and growth rate; you should also consider the coin's market capitalization.

Also consider the company's history and the currency's creators. Ensure that you enjoy what you read and that the developers are serious and supported by a robust team.

Consider visiting their website. Ensure that it appears professional, is well-written, and contains coherent information.

Whenever practicable, investigate the members of their development team and ensure they have relevant experience.

If possible, use their software and see if it works well. The currency will have a whitepaper; read it and see if you like what you read. See if there is any mention of the currency having security issues and if those issues have been resolved. Determine if the major cryptocurrency brokers and exchanges deal in the currency. If they do not investigate the reason,

Every day, new digital currencies are created.

Some have valid motivations for creation, while others only support those that do.

Currently, Bitcoin, Ethereum, Litecoin, and Ripple are some of the most prominent cryptocurrencies.

Before investing in a coin, thoroughly examine its history.

Before investing in a coin, make sure its circulating supply is not excessive.

Check the brokers and exchanges to assure the availability of the coin. If not, determine why.

Your fast start action step:

Using the processes outlined in this chapter, identify a coin that you believe is an investment opportunity. Then, either test it with a small investment or observe it for an extended period to determine whether it would have been a successful investment. You could do this for multiple cryptocurrencies if you so desired.

Emerging crypto-currencies

There are over a thousand cryptocurrencies, some of which are active and others inactive. New cryptocurrencies are entering the market and acquiring popularity as their market share continues to increase. In this section, we will examine the cryptocurrencies that investors and speculators must take into account.

The leading five emerging cryptocurrencies

Here are the top five emerging currencies:

Dash Dash is similar to Bitcoin but offers more privacy. It has a two-tiered network structure. The first framework is for miners who secure the network and add transactions to the blockchain. The second framework consists of 'masternodes' that transmit transactions and facilitate PrivateSend and InstantSend transactions.

PrivateSend is used for anonymous transactions, whereas InstantSend is used for private transactions.

Dash is the first decentralized autonomous organization due to its decentralized governance.

A master-node can be created by anyone who locks at least one thousand DASH coins on their server. Every master-node generates income for its operator. This encourages individuals to operate master-nodes, resulting in increased decentralization.

IOTA

As implied by its designation, IOTA is associated with IoT (Internet of Things). IOTA is thus a cryptocurrency designed for IoT. IOTA does not use distributed ledger technology. Instead, 'Tangle' is used. This allows it to reduce computational requirements and eradicate transaction fees.

Tangle requires the Sender of a transaction to perform a proof of work (PoW) that validates two separate transactions. This eliminates mining specialists from the system. This increases the system's decentralization as each user becomes a 'node' in the network.

Due to its Proof-of-Work (PoW) system, as more users conduct transactions, they also perform verification, thereby eliminating the congestion of verifications. Consequently, IOTA is inherently scalable.

NEO

Similar to Ethereum, NEO is a smart contract platform that enables the development of smart contracts and third-party distributed applications. The only distinction between NEO and Ethereum is that, unlike Ethereum, which requires developers to use 'Solidary' (a programming language similar to JavaScript), NEO allows developers to use any programming language they choose.

NEO is so ubiquitous in China that it has earned the moniker 'Chinese Etherium'.

Stellar Lumens

Stellar Lumens employs the identical principle as Ripples. Its monetary units are known as Lumens. Its goal is to become the cryptocurrency system of choice for banks and other financial institutions. Additionally, it aims to serve as a conduit between numerous other cryptocurrencies. Exchange platforms for cryptocurrencies are third-party 'anchors' that provide links between cryptocurrencies, allowing you to convert your transaction from one cryptocurrency to another. Stellar Lumens intends to implement the same concept, with the exception that these 'anchors' will reside on its network rather than on the networks of third parties.

Stellar Lumens appears optimistic, as it has partnered with IBM, one of the most prominent financial platform developers, to implement its concept. IBM is expected to own the custom blockchain solution for transaction clearing on its infrastructure, while transaction clearing will be performed on the Stellar Lumens network as part of this partnership. The partnership has bolstered Stellar Lumens' standing as a highly prospective and emerging competitor to Ripple.

Application of Blockchain to Finance

The application of blockchain technology to the Bitcoin system has piqued the interest of an increasing number of financial institutions.

Many operators in the financial sector, despite their reluctance towards Bitcoin, have studied the technology that governs its operation, recognizing its significance and revolutionary potential across multiple industries and processes, including the financial sector. Insights into the technological potential of blockchain have resulted in multimillion-dollar investments in R&D to acquire the knowledge necessary to develop their own P2P architecture.

The reasons relate to the various effects that technology would have on the financial market, such as reduced transaction costs and transaction times, the ability to quickly process information, and effects in terms of disintermediation in many processes where a "trust" authority seems unavoidable.

The above-described technological implications have the potential to revolutionize the entire financial system by applying blockchain to the operational core of financial institutions, such as currency transfers, payments, and stock market trading, as well as numerous other financial transactions.

Consider a cross-border transaction in which the transmission of funds between two parties is not only relatively expensive but also time-consuming.

By adopting a database, a ledger, based on blockchain technology, you could simultaneously reduce the transaction costs associated with the transfer and the time required to validate the transaction by eliminating the channels through which information flows to be validated.

From a traditional banking standpoint, transactions are stored on internal ledgers, and this can be done at different times by different banks, resulting in funds removed from one bank's ledger not appearing on another bank's ledger for several days.

By replacing traditional transaction authentication channels with the transparency of a distributed and shared ledger, which allows all network participants to read the transaction, blockchain technology enables the resolution of these issues.

The basic concept is that blockchain functionality can be used to record, verify, and transfer any form of contract or property, thereby displacing the need for numerous brokerage services. Clearly, currencies and payments are the first and most apparent application of finance, but they do not exhaust the field.

In fact, innovation can be applied to numerous categories of financial transactions, such as reinventing the stock market, private equity, the bond market, investment instruments, and derivatives.

Numerous institutions within the banking industry are preparing for the technological revolution by investing primarily in research to assess the impact on their business models and secondarily in diverse application projects to leverage the technological wave.

One example is Deutsche Bank, which in 2015 transformed its interest in the technology into a project consisting of the launch of several Innovation Labs with the goal of accelerating the global development of the fintech sector and blockchain startups.

The fintech company R3 Cev tested the validity and efficacy of issuing, marketing, and redeeming a corporate bond using a shared blockchain ledger in another significant initiative. Banks such as Bank of America, Banco Santander, Goldman Sachs, J.P. Morgan, and a number of others participated in the initiative by contributing their cloud computing and data mining services.

Even on the stock and bond markets, blockchain technology may revolutionize transactions. On December 30, 2015, NASDAQ, the primary index of technology stocks on the U.S. stock exchange, launched NASDAQ Linq, a blockchain-based bond trading service. The purpose of this service is to expedite settlements on public markets.

Subsequently, NASDAQ Linq has also targeted the equity sector, specifically for pre-IPO transactions, testing the trading of private company shares via a distributed ledger containing all the information currently managed through conventional means.

Therefore, the subject of these blockchain-based transactions are shares of stock in private companies prior to their initial public offering.

This mechanism eliminates the need for a variety of intermediaries, such as legal counsel, auditors, consultants, and bookkeepers, in the pre-IPO phase.

The NASDAQ Linq application, operating as a digital ledger, will provide a record of every stock transfer between blockchain users, thereby streamlining controls and increasing the transparency of stock transactions.

NASDAQ, Citibank, Visa, and Capital One have invested over $30 million in Chain.com for the implementation of distributed ledgers to manage interbank transactions.

"Blockchain technology continues to redefine not only how the stock market industry operates, but also the global financial economy as a whole," said Bob Greifeld8.

The P2P currency system (transactional application)

The first stable global application of blockchain technology was in the field of transactions, due to its implementation in the Bitcoin system, which was described by its anonymous creator as "A Peer-to-Peer Electronic Cash System". It is essential to keep in mind that "Distributed Ledger Transaction" is merely one of the applications derived from the blockchain; it is a common error to mistake a component of the whole for the whole itself.

The blockchain enables the creation of a database for the management of transactions that have transpired between network nodes. In summary, it is a database composed of blocks containing various transactions that are interconnected so that each transaction that occurs on the network is approved by its nodes. This mechanism enables the creation of a transparently traceable archive for each transaction. (Figure 7)

Figure 7: How Blockchain transactions operate

Having previously addressed the various stages that characterize a BTC transaction between two hypothetical network nodes (Bob and Alice), this section will discuss some additional concepts and effects related to a transaction in the Bitcoin system.

Given that, in this context, a transaction is a transfer that is broadcast to the entire network and recorded in a given block of the blockchain, it is important to note that each transaction can consist of multiple inputs and outputs.

Inputs are nothing more than references to previous transactions' outputs. In reality, a Bitcoin address that has received n payments contains n outputs that can be used in subsequent transactions. This establishes a genuine remainders and fees system.

We investigate two cases.

In the first scenario, which is considered the default case, a user who has previously received, say, 5 BTC must pay back the same amount in a transaction. In this instance, the input of the transaction will contain the ID of the prior output (of 5 BTC previously received by a single output) along with the address of the payment recipient and the amount to be sent (always 5 BTC). In this trivial scenario, all of the user's Bitcoins are transferred to the recipient.

If the BTC to be sent are not all of the user's BTC, but only a portion, the situation is drastically different. Considering the input/output system as blocks of Bitcoins divisible only by transactions, the blocks must be incorporated in their entirety into the transaction, preventing the sending of only a portion of the Bitcoins owned.

Returning to the example, if the user were to transmit only 3 of the 5 BTC he possessed, he would still be required to transfer all 5 BTC. To circumvent this issue, a remainder address is employed, i.e., an additional address pertaining to the user who initiated the transaction is added to the transaction's output, to which the remaining BTC are sent.

The BTC of change does not go back to the user if they do not provide a change address. Instead, it is deemed a transaction cost and is earned by the "Miners" who verified the transaction.

This complicated procedure is frequently simplified by software that manages Bitcoin wallets and automatically generates an address to which the excess quantity of cryptocurrency should be sent.

The issue of "Double Spending" (in the case of Bitcoin).

Without the need for a central authority, the complete Bitcoin system is managed by a database that is replicated across all nodes and records and archives all digital currency exchanges. Speaking of digital, consider a digital file, which, if copied, cannot be distinguished from the original file due to the fact that both are constituted of bits.

Transferring this logic to the Bitcoin system, we refer to double spending when it is possible to spend the same "digital token" twice or more, considering this phenomenon to be the most crucial aspect of digital currencies.

As a decentralized system, Bitcoin relies on the integrity of the network node-miners who verify and validate transactions ("Miners") to function.

A node-miner is considered honest if it employs its computational capacity to generate blocks that do not contain transactions that are inconsistent, contradictory, or previously recorded on the blockchain.

When a malicious network node pursues the fraudulent goal of spending the same unit of digital currency multiple times, double spending occurs.

This issue should be resolved through the proper maintenance of the blockchain, an immutable and shared ledger that uses a time stamp to imprint each block, i.e., a specific sequence of characters that uniquely and irrevocably identifies a date/time stamp to confirm the actual occurrence of an event.

Each timestamp contains and retains the previous one in its hash form, thereby creating a chain, the Blockchain.

However, this mechanism does not safeguard the system against assaults such as double spending. As for the technical details, when a new block of transactions is deliberated and approved by the miners, the transactions contained within it are authorized once, and by adding more blocks, you receive additional confirmations for the transactions contained within the previous blocks.

Due to the prospect of blockchain bifurcations, a transaction cannot be deemed unrelated to the phenomenon of double spending until it has received a sufficient number of confirmations.

Consider the scenario in which a malicious network node initiates two transactions using the same unit of digital currency almost simultaneously. There are two transactions in this case: A and B.

As soon as the malicious node initiates operation A, it will be deposited in a block on the blockchain and become visible to the recipient, who will therefore receive an initial confirmation.

Before transaction A is placed in a block, the node could secretly create another block containing transaction B, which transmits the same BTC to a different address, thereby rendering transaction A invalid.

However, the malicious node will not communicate transaction B to the network, only transaction A, because if it did, the other nodes would notice the difference between the two transactions, and the recipient of the payment would discover the deception when he or she does not receive confirmation for transaction A.

By not communicating the resolution of a block to the other miners (transaction B), the honest miners will continue to develop the public chain, whereas the malicious node will generate new blocks to attach to its private chain (chain B of Figure 8), with the intention of releasing it into the network when it will be longer than the public chain, thereby becoming the dominant chain. The transactions enclosed within the orphaned blocks are invalid. It is challenging to implement this strategy, but it is possible by identifying a system flaw.

The double spending attack is a race between the malicious node and the rest of the network to generate additional blocks beginning with the current one before transaction A is approved.

Even if the likelihood of such an attack is remote, it will succeed if the malicious node alone possesses a computational capacity that is greater than fifty percent plus one percent of the network's total computational capacity.

It is necessary to specify, for the sake of completeness, that when referring to computing capacity, the hash rate is expressed as a percentage. This indicates the number of hashes that a device is capable of generating per second. For instance, 1GH / s corresponds to the capacity to generate 1 billion hashes per second.

The framework of the units

As previously stated, the blockchain consists of a collection of blocks comprising a certain number of interconnected transactions. This enables the construction of a shared ledger containing a record of all system-approved transactions that have occurred.

It is necessary to describe the articulation of each block in greater detail.

Each block consists of two fundamental components: the block header and the list of transactions contained within the block9. Let's conduct a detailed analysis.

Block Header

It contains various information and serves as the block's identification document:

Block number or height: represents the increasing number of blocks added to a chain. The initial block of a blockchain is referred to as the genesis block and is associated with the number zero.

Hash: is the identification code of a specific block and is derived from the hashing of various information such as the version number of the verification software used in the protocol, the hash of the previous block so that it is linked, the time the block was resolved, the Merkle root, the memory used, and the nonce (concepts that will be discussed in greater detail below).

The hash of the prior block contains all information about the previous block.

The next block's hash, which is only visible if the block has been added to the chain.

The timestamp contains the date and time the obstruction was resolved.

Difficulty: understood as the processing time required to solve the cryptographic problem in the mining process. It is the difficulty of solving the obstacle, or validating and recording it.

Transactions: The number of transactions included within the block.

Total BTC: This value represents the total amount of Bitcoins sent across all transactions in the block, including transaction fees.

Size: indicates how much memory is occupied by all transaction data in the block.

Merkle Root: represents the hash that synthesizes all transactions within the block, where each transaction represents a "Merkle Tree" leaf.

Nonce: (number used once) guarantees that the data in the block cannot be reused, for example in a cyber-attack, but it will be treated more precisely later.

It represents a schema in which all transactions included in the block are listed, along with their respective hashes, fees, memory usage, and addresses.

It is also essential to note that the first transaction in a block list is referred to as a "coinbase." This, placed in the block by the winning miner, the one who first solved the block, creates brand new Bitcoins (currency creation) payable to that miner as a reward for having solved the block or validated and approved the transactions in it, thus carrying out the activity of "Mining," which will be analyzed in detail in the following section.

Mining For Consensus In A Trustless Network

In the blockchain, consensus refers to the process of validating and verifying transactions using the computing capacity provided by network participants.

This computational power enables the system to rely on a decentralized and distributed consensus, as opposed to the consensus that would be formed in the presence of a centralized guarantor institution.

"Miners" refers to network nodes that actively participate in solving cryptographic riddles and validating blocks of transactions. Miners are compensated with the creation of new digital currency for undertaking a resource-intensive activity. The rationale behind the consensus/approval mechanism derives from the need to create obstacles and complications during the validation process in order to prevent deception attempts by the P2P network's nodes.

Computer-mathematical problems are designed to pit all nodes against one another as they compete to solve the problem with their computing capacity.

The first node to solve the cryptographic conundrum and present the solution to the network will earn the privilege of validating the block of transactions.

The effort expended in solving the issue and the resulting solution determine the miner's compensation in digital currency, as well as the emission and creation of new digital currency.

The consensus procedure, incentives, and costs of Bitcoin mining.

The Bitcoin system's most significant innovation is the decentralized consensus mechanism. In this instance, we use the term "emergent consent" because the consent is not acquired explicitly and there is no set time when it will be obtained.

Instead, consensus is reached through the asynchronous interaction of a large number of nodes (P2P network users) that approve and adhere to the rules on which the computer protocol that manages transactions is based.

Importantly, Bitcoin, its properties, transactions, and system security are all derived from the decentralized consensus mechanism. Every transaction initiated in the system is disclosed on Bitcoin's P2P network, but it does not become part of the shared ledger until it has been verified and added to a blockchain via mining.

This process serves two crucial Bitcoin system functions:

The mining procedure generates new Bitcoins by validating transaction blocks added to the blockchain. The creation of new currency serves the purpose of compensating miners for their work validating and approving transactions.

Mining fosters confidence by tying the confirmation of transactions to the use of sufficient computing power to verify the block containing them. In this context, it is essential to note that the number of nodes in the chain determines the amount of computing power required for the approval mechanism, thereby increasing system integrity.

As mentioned previously, the mining process determines the addition of new Bitcoin to the circulating digital currency. In addition, this activity provides protection against fraudulent transactions, such as the previously described phenomenon of double spending.

Miners perform these tasks by contributing computational power to the Bitcoin network in the hopes of receiving compensation.

To partake in mining, it is necessary to connect to the Bitcoin network by downloading software that implements this protocol and enables the execution of cryptographic mining operations.

Every 10 minutes, on average, a new block containing the transactions that occurred in the system after the resolution of the previous block is deemed "mined" or resolved and is subsequently added to the blockchain ledger.

This requirement is stipulated by the Bitcoin system's operational protocol.

Therefore, transactions contained in the "resolved" block added to the registry are deemed valid, allowing new BTC owners to expend them in subsequent transactions.

For their participation in the approval/consent mechanism, network nodes (Miners) receive two types of rewards.

As soon as a block is confirmed and uploaded to the blockchain, new BTCs are generated.

The second is the transaction fees for all transactions within a block.

Miners compete to solve a complex math-computer problem based on a cryptographic hashing algorithm in order to earn these rewards.

The solution to this problem represents the miner's proof of work, demonstrating that sufficient computing power was utilized.

Similar to the mining of precious metals, the process of creating new cryptocurrencies follows a downward trend.

In fact, the money supply created by the mining process, which accounts for a portion of the miners' reward, decreases approximately every four years, or more precisely, whenever 210,000 resolved blocks are added to the Bitcoin blockchain.

In practice, Bitcoin generation began in 2009 with the creation of 50 BTC per solved block, halved to 25 BTC in November 2012, and reached 12.5 BTC in 2016, the current reward for the miner who successfully solves the cryptographic puzzle.

By continuing this process, the reward of mining in the Bitcoin system and, consequently, the creation of new currency will decrease exponentially until the year 2140, when the maximum of 21 million Bitcoins will have been issued. Regarding mining activity compensation, the probability of obtaining it, and thus solving the blockchain, is proportional to the ratio between the computational power of each individual node and the total power of the network.

As of today, transaction fees account for less than 0.5% of a miner's total earnings, as the vast majority of rewards are derived from the creation of new currency. The largest portion of a miner's earnings, however, will consist of transaction fees. This is due to the fact that the latter type of reward is decreasing over time and that Bitcoin system developments will increase the size (in bytes) of each block, allowing it to contain a greater number of transactions.

In fact, after the year 2140, when the minting of new cryptocurrencies will cease, the only source of income for miners will be transaction fees, with revenues dependent on the Bitcoin system's penetration of the payment market.

In a sense, the term mining is misleading because it transfers the emphasis to the process of creating new money, which is merely a reward for hard work.

Rather, the primary objective of such activity is to establish a consensus mechanism that results in the approval of transactions, thereby securing the entire Bitcoin system.

The incentive scheme is merely a tool for aligning the objective function of each network node-miner with the stability and security of the P2P computer protocol, thereby incentivizing the integrity of the nodes that safeguard the registry from those who would alter it (dishonest nodes).

In order to examine mining activity in the Bitcoin system in greater detail, it is essential to note that, according to the protocol's rules, regardless of the number of transactions initiated in the network, an average of 2,016 new blocks must be generated every two weeks, or one block every 10 minutes.

It is essential to discuss the existence of a rebalancing mechanism when designating 2,016 new blocks to be produced every 14 days as the target number (target). In actuality, the difficulty of solving the cryptographic conundrum, i.e. the difficulty of producing a new block, is modified every two weeks if the number of transaction blocks produced deviates from the target number (2,016). If the number is less than the goal, the difficulty will be adjusted downward; if the number is greater than the goal, the difficulty will be increased.

Given the intense competition among nodes to find the solution to the cryptographic puzzle, it is natural to anticipate an increase in the network's computational capacity (hash-rate)[10]over time, followed by a parallel increase in the difficulty required of miners to solve the cryptographic problem.

In reality, the difficulty varies based on the network's total computational capacity, so that each block is generated on average every 10 minutes. Analyzing the process from a procedural standpoint, whenever Bitcoin network transactions are initiated and detected by nodes, if they are not in conflict with other transactions, they are deposited in a temporary pool of unverified transactions. Each individual node that stores the complete transaction history (blockchain) maintains this pool.

All miners attempting to generate a new block will utilize this pool by inserting the unverified transactions contained within it into the new block they are working on individually. In other words, they will attempt to solve a challenging cryptographic problem, known as "proof of work," in order to validate the block of transactions and add it to the blockchain ledger.

Each miner will attempt to discover the solution to validate the block and claim the reward by adding transactions based on criteria such as the highest associated fee (commission).

As each new block builds on the previous block via a cascade of digital signatures, the insertion of additional blocks and the resolution of additional puzzles will increase confidence and consensus in previously inserted blocks.

Before moving on to the analysis of mining costs, which will be covered in the following section, it is important to recall that the Bitcoin network exploits the computational power derived from the hardware devices made available by the network's nodes.

Initially, CPUs were used for mining, but these have since been supplanted by 3D graphics cards comparable to those used in video games. ASICS are the most prevalent systems of this type. This change is due to the fact that the second system performs more operations per unit of energy consumed than the first. In reality, the disparity between CPUs and 3D graphics cards in terms of energy consumption to "extract" the same quantity of Bitcoin is quite large, to the detriment of the former.

Based on what has been said, it is necessary to introduce a second cost component to mining, namely energy consumption. However, this factor is subject to significant variation based on the country in which mining will occur, allowing for geographical arbitrage.

Financial Indicators

In the coming years, experts predict that trading in cryptocurrencies will be dominated by algorithms and artificial intelligence. Since stocks and commodities have begun using Quants or Quantitative Analysis, there is no doubt. Quants are comparable to technical traders in that they employ statistical and mathematical trading strategies. You don't need to be a mathematician to learn how to trade, so don't fret.

You should begin acquiring it immediately so that you can remain competitive. It is essential to learn and comprehend technical analysis and how to use the program to aid in cryptocurrency trading. Consider that cryptocurrencies lend themselves naturally to program trading.

Initially, you must be aware of the four market zones. The first market zone is the Japanese time zone, which runs from 8 p.m. to 4 p.m. Eastern Standard Time. You receive a reasonable amount of volume during this time. The Middle East Market follows, beginning around midnight EST and concluding at 8 am EST. It overlaps with the European Market until 10 a.m. EST, when the US East Coast begins to increase the volume, and continues until 8 p.m. EST because of the West Coast.

When conducting business, you must be aware of prime hours. If you don't have an AI monitor to monitor the volumes, you can use these market zones in your program to assume that these are the peak hours – particularly if there is an overlap between the market zones, as you are assured of a higher volume and have a better chance of using statistical and computational strategies. Peak overlap business hours result in increased volume and market volatility, resulting in greater profits.

Moving Averages

Moving Averages (MA) are the simplest and most effective instrument for obtaining a technical education when you have a complex system or choose to run the numbers manually. You'll get forms like MA-30, MA-5, etc. The number represents the duration over which the average is calculated. Using MA-30 as an illustration, it represents the 30-period moving average of values.

We chose "periods" rather than "days" because you will determine the time scale. The time scale for short-term trades can be as brief as 30 seconds, 1 minute, or 5 minutes. If you are interested in a long-term investment, you can use days. Additionally, you can use them to comprehend the longer-term trend and the short-term fluctuations.

For instance, a 30-day moving average can be used to determine the long-term trend. Additionally, this reveals your bias. Consequently, if the trajectory indicated an upward movement, you will have a bias that prices will rise, and you should favor long positions (buy positions). If the long-term trajectory is falling, you should have a preference for short positions (selling positions).

Typically, two long-term trends, such as MA-35 and MA-21, which will be measured in days, can be utilized. This results in a long-term bias. We will therefore utilize short-term indicators such as the MA-3 and MA-8, which will be measured in minutes. Taking the price at the end of a minute three times in a row, adding them together, and then dividing by three. For instance, the price at 9:01 am is 10, the price at 9:02 am is 10.5, and the price at 9:03 am is 10.8. You will therefore select 10, 10.5, and 10.8. When you add them up you'll get 31.2. Next, divide 31.2 by 3 (since there are three periods) to obtain 10.4. Now we can state that MA3 is 31.2. The following step is to plot this line and then overlay it on the price chart. There is a chart that smooths out the price movement. When you superimpose the MA-8, which is the eight-period moving average, you will obtain two lines that are likely to flow together.

The signal will be generated when one line crosses another. For instance, when MA-3 is below MA-8, a downward trend is indicated. When MA-3 is above MA-8, however, this indicates an upward trend. This will function as your indicator for the short term.

Likewise, the same holds true for your long-term indicator. The long-term indicator (measured in days) reveals a longer-term trend and can serve as the basis for your extended bias. If your long-term trend demonstrates an upward trajectory, this will become your long bias. Therefore, if you have a long bias necessitated by the longer MA and the shorter MA indicates the short-term trend, you are in an excellent position to scalp the market in either direction.

Here is how to accomplish that:

When the long-term moving average has a long bias, you must focus on the fact that the market will soon turn up, so you can begin with a buy position. As soon as the short-term indicator displays a buy signal, you must immediately enter the market. When the short-term indicator changes to a sell signal, you can liquidate your current position and initiate a new short position. Nevertheless, this second short position is to be more sensitive. At the first instance of the short-term changing back to the buy, the position must be liquidated, the profit taken, and then a new buy position opened. You should continue doing this each time an opportunity presents itself, particularly if a large number arises during peak market hours. With a liquid market, you can derive the greatest benefit from this indicator.

Traders with extensive experience consider this an outstanding indicator. Moreover, this is the only indicator that is suitable for uncomplicated markets and can generate profits. If you decide to experiment with program trades, which you should do, you can use the app's test feature to evaluate the strategy on historical price movements and examine the trade signals.

Explicit Moving Average

In some markets, such as the BTC-USD (Bitcoin-U.S. Dollar) rates, the exponential moving average or EMA is utilized more frequently because it is more efficient. The only difference between EMA and MA is that the weight is applied to various periods. The explanation is that the number that is closest to the present should contribute more to the average than the number that is further back in time. There are numerous benefits to utilizing this calculation. It functions well for Bitcoin-Ethereum (BTC-ETH) exchanges and other crypto-crypto rates.

EMA performs better in markets with less volatility because the results tend to be more sensitive, leading to a rise in false positives.

You can enhance the counter by adjusting the weights of the prices. Additionally, you can use the EMA13 and EMA21 horizons. When these two horizons intersect, it will signify whether to buy or sell.

When the quicker horizon is higher, it indicates that it's time to buy. When the slower horizon is higher, it indicates a sale signal. This can be used in conjunction with the standard moving average for other counters. It may function with less volatile pairs, such as Ripple versus Monero or Ethereum versus Ripple.

ADX Indicators

Before moving on to the final indicator, it is crucial to note that profiting in crypto trading does not require identifying trends in price movements, but rather turning points. You can expect greater profits if you correctly identify the point where a turn is most likely to occur, so you should disregard false positives.

When you are ultimately trading, enter at the beginning of a run and continue scalping small price fluctuations. This is the reason why a 24-hour market is superior, as it allows for continuous data analysis. There are no sudden begins and stops between the end of one session and the beginning of the next. Instead of leaving open positions unattended, it is prudent to liquidate and square your positions at the end of each trading day, particularly if you do not have an AI engine or an online program.

On the price chart, a line chart represents the ADX indicator. Price charts typically depict price fluctuations, providing visual signals for manual work and the conception of strategies. Typically, online programs do not recognize chart presentation, but rather equations, data, and variables. The majority of experienced traders prefer the visual representation because it provides a clearer image of the positions and movements.

It is unnecessary to learn precisely how to calculate the ADX because it is of little use if it is not analyzed in real-time in order to easily assess how the trading day is progressing. In addition, the majority of online trading portals will perform the calculation and provide the result promptly.

ADX calculation knowledge is less essential than understanding how to maximize usage.

With the ADX plotting in real-time at the bottom of the chart, you receive a statistic supporting another, and the moving averages are clearly visible on the price chart. The ADX provides insight into the momentum of the counter or move. The counter is between 0 and 100. The percentage of strength is the information obtained. Data above 80 indicates a significant moment in a particular trend, whereas data below 30 indicates little to no momentum. When the ADX line crosses the 30% line, momentum will begin to increase, as indicated by overlapping MA. This represents your confidence in the signals.

It requires greater labor and effort than usual, but it may be worthwhile. This is most useful when you reach the portion of a trading program where the momentum is automatically checked to determine if a trade is feasible. Therefore, when you begin using algorithms to telegraph your trades, you must familiarize yourself with ADX so that you can adjust the parameters for optimal results.

The Prospects For Cryptocurrency

As soon as cryptocurrencies enter the picture, global divisions emerge. Bill Gates, Al Gore, and Richard Branson are among the proponents who believe cryptocurrencies are superior to conventional currencies. Included among those who disagree are Warren Buffet, Paul Krugman, and Robert Shiller. Krugman and Shiller, Nobel laureates in economics, refer to it as a Ponzi scheme and a method of perpetrating a crime.

In the future, there will be a conflict between regulation and anonymity. A number of cryptocurrencies have been linked to terrorist activity, so governments would want to supervise how they operate. The primary objective of cryptocurrencies, on the other hand, is to preserve user anonymity.

By 2030, futurists predict that cryptocurrencies will account for 25 percent of all national currencies, indicating that a significant portion of the global population will begin using them for commerce. It will continue to have a volatile nature, which means that prices will fluctuate as they have for the past several years, and it will be tolerated by businesses and consumers to an increasing degree.

Why is cryptocurrency the future of finance?

Cryptocurrencies, the first alternative to the current financial system, have numerous advantages over previous payment methods and conventional asset classes. Examine them Money 2.0 is a brand-new form of currency that is exclusive to the internet and has the potential to become the world's quickest, simplest, cheapest, safest, and most widely used method of exchanging value.

Cryptocurrencies cannot be regulated by a central authority because none exists; they can be used as payment for goods and services or as an investment asset.

Your cryptocurrency funds will be safe regardless of what a government does. Regardless of your country of origin or current domicile, digital currencies guarantee opportunity equality. As long as you own a smartphone or other internet-connected device, you have the same access to crypto as everyone else. Cryptocurrencies offer unique opportunities for enhancing the economic liberty of individuals worldwide. The inherent borderlessness of digital currencies facilitates free trade, especially in nations with stringent cash controls. In nations where inflation is a significant concern, cryptocurrencies may provide a viable alternative to failing fiat currencies for savings and payments.

As part of a larger investment strategy, cryptocurrency can be approached in a variety of methods. A bitcoin, which was practically worthless in 2008 but now sells for hundreds of dollars per coin, is one option. A different strategy would be to adopt a more proactive posture and actively purchase and sell volatile cryptocurrencies.

The 1:1 pegged USD Coin to the value of the U.S. dollar is an option for crypto-curious investors seeking to reduce risk. It combines the stability of a conventional currency with the advantages of cryptocurrencies, most notably the quick and inexpensive transmission of funds across international borders. Users of Coin Base with USDC are rewarded, making it an attractive alternative to a conventional savings account.

Why should you purchase digital currencies?

Thanks to online exchanges like Coinbase, buying and selling cryptocurrencies is now straightforward, secure, and lucrative. After establishing a secure account, you can purchase cryptocurrencies using your debit card or bank account. Because fractional coins are available, you can purchase as little (or as much) cryptocurrency as you desire. For example, you could purchase $25 worth of bit money.

Numerous digital currencies, including USD Coin and Tezos, provide their owners with rewards simply for retaining them. On a Coin basis, you can earn 1% APY, which is significantly higher than the vast majority of conventional savings accounts. When staking Tezos per coin, it is possible to earn up to 5% APY. Learn more about Tezos staking reward information. In contrast to stocks and bonds, you can rapidly transfer cryptocurrency to anyone and use it to purchase products and services. Bitcoin and other digital currencies are included in the investment portfolios of millions of individuals.

Investments In Distributed Video Streaming

The global market for real-time video is exploding. Content such as web recordings, films, television, and YouTube recordings are crucial to this 50 billion dollar industry that is expected to grow by 20% annually over the next decade. Demand for increased quantities of this content is increasing, but so is the number of users experiencing streaming issues. This is due to the fact that our current integrated video delivery systems are no longer sufficient. To remain relevant with consumers, video web-based platforms and providers must evolve and decentralize. Theta is currently the leader in the decentralized video web space and blockchain is one of the developments they're pursuing. Theta is a digital currency initiative that has been in the news for the proper reasons. Over the past year, Theta has made tremendous strides in reception, obtained numerous high-profile partnerships, and released a series of convention enhancements that could forever alter the video real time world. In the following section, I will discuss a few of these new accomplishments and why I believe Theta's finest days are ahead. Theta is a blockchain-powered decentralized real-time feature developed by Theta Labs, a Californian technology company with South Korean roots. Theta believes that its exceptional plan can guarantee steady, high-quality video transmissions in 4k and 8k resolutions more efficiently and with more real-time features. Theta achieves this through communication and innovation.

Utilizing a network of local hubs that reserve video data and give off transfers to viewers, video transfers can be accomplished at a reduced cost. To encourage individuals to reserve and transmit video content, Theta compensates network members with cryptographic currency, specifically its T-fuel token. The T-fuel token is used to pay for transaction fees on the Theta blockchain and can be freely traded on multiple exchanges. T-fuel is comparable to Theta's representation of gas on Ethereum. Intriguingly, the Theta token, which has been symbolic since the March fire, is used for identification and administration on the Theta organization. Despite the fact that designating awards on Theta is not particularly valuable, more than fifty percent of Theta's entire stock is currently being marked by more than three thousand hubs around the world - a strong indication of assistance with the mission. Both T-fuel and Theta are native to the Theta blockchain, which employs a byzantine open-minded agreement component with staggered byzantine shortcoming. The Theta blockchain is renowned for its astounding efficiency, with an average transaction time of just.

3 seconds, with the option to handle over 1,000 transactions per second. The year 2020 has been a busy one for Theta. Theta released Theta Live Embed, which enables websites, blogs, and surprisingly web-based media platforms to broadcast content from Theta.tv, which was primarily E-Sports at the time. Decorations, observers, and the site facilitating the stream would each receive 33 percent of the T-fuel produced by the stream. Assuming one million people view a Theta broadcast, this could pay anywhere from fifty to one hundred thousand dollars to the site and, presumably, a similar amount to the streamer and viewers combined. The first company to integrate Theta Live Embed onto their website was GFuel, a popular energy drink among gamers. In April, Theta began to differentiate the content on Theta.tv by adding a 24x7 poker stream in collaboration with global poker visit. On the sixth of May, Theta announced that they had collaborated with Coindesk to be the

recipient of the agreement's elite decoration, which included the most prominent names in the crypto sector. The next day, Theta sent out the Theta.tv android application that was compatible with smart televisions. This enables any smart TV to become a relayer node for the Theta organization, sharing transfer speed and stream optimization with nearby viewers. Theta also announced that they would make the Theta SDK used to build the Android application available to all developers, making it easy for Netflix and YouTube to incorporate the Theta protocol into their broadcasts. This action appears to have caught the attention of Google, which joined Theta and became a validator on the Theta blockchain shortly thereafter. That day, Theta's mainnet 2.0 was officially launched. In addition to enhancing the company's presentation, Theta announced that watchman hubs would have the option to participate in block creation - a function that had previously been restricted to enterprise-run validator hubs. This is crucial because it significantly increased the decentralization of the Theta blockchain. During this period, Theta also collaborated with MGM Studios to stream classic Hollywood films on Theta.tv throughout the middle of the year. All of these announcements were made in the same week that Samsung announced that Theta.tv broadcasts would be integrated into Samsung Daily, which is currently available on more than 75 million Samsung mobile devices. Before the end of May, the number of nodes on the Theta network had multiplied, and the cost of Theta token on certain exchanges had increased fivefold, from a dime to more than 50 pennies. However, this was only the beginning of Theta's upward trend. Expanding on the momentum from May, Theta announced an optimistic advancement plan in June. The principal accomplishments they detailed incorporated the presentation of smart contracts with the specific objective of supervising protected content on their site and creating a prophet for their organization to give content creators, publicists, and distributors clarity. Evidently Theta wasn't joking, as a June report on blockchain development by exception adventures found that Theta had a 10x increase in development activity in the second quarter of 2020, making it the third most utilized digital currency in that period. This report likely spread at Coinbase due to their July announcement that Theta was one of the cryptocurrencies they were considering listing. In August, Fail Army became Theta.tv's first premium content partner. Theta labs also announced that, despite having sufficient funds to continue development, they would open and sell 30 million of their branded Theta tokens to add more vitality to their development. Then, in September, Theta disclosed that a portion of their accelerated momentum involved attempting to carve out a niche in the DeFi space. To this end, they revealed that Theta smart contracts will be interoperable with Ethereum smart contracts. Then Theta announced that their decentralized streaming protocol had been granted an American patent. As expected, this substantial patent establishes Theta network as the only successful blockchain-based decentralized video convention. Theta joined forces with Chainlink to identify malicious streams, such as crypto trick streams, as the icing on the cake. In November, Theta announced the beta release of Theta Edgecast, the first completely decentralized web-based video convention. It is constructed entirely on the Theta blockchain using smart contracts, without the use of a centralized server or support. Despite the fact that December has only just begun, Theta has already made additional monumental declarations. Theta.tv now features a K-pop diversion channel, and Smart agreements on Theta are now active. The December tenth overhauls of Theta are enormous for the undertaking. Assuming you already own Theta, T-fuel tokens, or are a center for the Theta organization, you need not worry about a hard fork with these updates. But what precisely will Theta alter? Initially, it will facilitate smart contracts on the Theta blockchain, which has been in development for months. Theta smart contracts will be interoperable with Ethereum smart contracts, and both Theta Labs and members of the Theta community are currently building DEXs, marking pools, and other DAPps that will go live on Theta in the coming months. Theta will also have its own fungible and non-fungible symbolic guidelines, allowing for the creation of new resources and NFT collectibles.

Theta. This is crucial given Theta's strong ties to the E-Sports industry. Utilizing decentralized applications necessitates a wallet extension like

Metamask. Overall, Theta has developed a program module that resembles Metamask and will serve as the central repository for all Theta-related information. Not only can you mint new tokens using Theta's new wallet expansion, but you'll also be able to use Theta's existing web wallet to easily create new smart contracts. Theta has also redesigned the Theta blockchain explorer, which they introduced after the well-known Ethereum blockchain explorer, Etherscan.io, in order to monitor this large number of new resources and dazzling contracts. Theta has reduced the stake required to become a watchman validator for their organization from 10,000 Theta tokens to only 1,000 Theta tokens, but this is by no means the last change. This is essential for Theta's ongoing efforts to further decentralize the Theta environment, which Theta Labs intends to eventually convert into a decentralized, community-run organization. What specific plans does

Theta have for the foreseeable future, and how will this affect the price of the Theta token? Indeed, Theta does not yet have a clearly defined plan for 2021, but recent meetings with Wes Levitt, Theta Labs' chief of methodology, have provided us with a few hints. Prioritatively, Theta laboratories remains hyper-focused on development and believes it can continue securing large partnerships for the next few years. Wes indicated that Theta's strategy is not to seize the streaming industry by force, but rather to establish footholds in the various specialties of video real time. This is confirmed by the indisputably unique content being added to Theta.tv. Instead of coming in and guaranteeing partners the world over, Theta intends to demonstrate that their technology works admirably and will significantly enhance their customers' experiences, as well as how much annual profit they're able to generate. Theta Labs is so intent on developing relationships in the streaming industry that they remain in California despite the more favorable economic conditions offered by Fintech and cryptocurrency hubs such as Switzerland. Second, it is evident that Theta intends to interfere with the DeFi space. Whether they intend to take a portion of Ethereum's market share is currently unknown, but I believe this drive is an effort to bring issues with the project to light and attract more customers to the Theta ecosystem. Unfortunately, Theta.tv's commitment has been disappointing thus far. Whether or not Theta's financial tricks will endeavor to acquire bodies is currently unknown, but whatever gets people talking about Theta will undoubtedly be adequate for the job.

entails forcing DeFi's honey bees out of their hive. Theta laboratories desires to decentralize its organization to the greatest extent possible and ultimately transform Theta into a decentralized independent organization. It is not entirely clear to me how they intend to accomplish this, nor is it entirely clear how Theta's current administration system operates. Theta ought to be an administration token, but a portion of Theta's only existing documentation regarding legislatures suggests that voting should be restricted to large business validator centers such as Google and Binance. I should also observe that I'm not entirely convinced that transitioning to a decentralized independent organization is the best course of action for Theta. This will fundamentally depend on how Theta's administration operates and how it may alter as the project becomes more decentralized. I expect administration to be the primary focus for Theta in 2021. Theta issued a statement regarding mainnet 3.0, which is anticipated to launch in the spring of 2021. This will provide the organization with Elite Edge hubs, which are created when a standard edge hub is fueled with T-fuel. In addition to T-fuel marking, T-fuel consumption will be introduced.

Twenty-five percent of all T-fuel deposits made in the edge network that powers Theta's edge vehicle streaming convention will be consumed. However, what will the price of Theta and T-fuel be? Well, analyzing Theta and T-fuel are two entirely distinct things due to the fact that Theta and T-fuel have vastly different tokenomics and use cases. Theta is used for branding and administration, while T-fuel is used to pay for transactions on the Theta blockchain. Theta stakers acquire T-fuel, which is also distributed to viewers, content creators, and websites facilitating Theta-based broadcasts. Beginning in the spring of 2021, T-fuel will also be stakeable and there will be some consumption for network fees. As you can imagine, this T-fuel technology necessitates a particular type of tokenomics that is not ideal for rewarding activity. While Theta has a maximum supply of one billion, T-fuel has a base supply of five billion and is also inflationary. The expansion of T-fuel does not appear to have begun yet, but when it does, its stock will increase at a rate of approximately 5% per year or as required by the Theta organization. Worse yet, Theta marking rewards are low in comparison to other digital currencies, yielding only one percent per year, which is unexpectedly good news for T-fuel. Unfortunately, the introduction of T-fuel consumption in 2021 will likely not be sufficient to counterbalance the expansion of the symbolic will insight. In addition, because T-fuel is a marking reward, there will always be a much higher level of sell pressure for the T-fuel token than for the Theta token. Despite the fact that T-fuel is currently siphoning, I hold a very negative view of it.

Nonetheless, I believe Theta can and will continue to experience tremendous growth. Reducing the marketing advantage from 10,000 to 1,000 Theta may be sufficient to entice individuals to purchase and invest in Theta. While there does not appear to be a restriction period for the Theta token, something tells me that the most invested venture validators will not be withdrawing their stakes in the near future. Significantly, we are approaching the beginning of the next crypto bull run. Theta arose well after the conclusion of the previous bull run and only became its own token in 2019. Although this makes it difficult to predict how high Theta could go, the lack of opposition in the past leads me to believe that anything is possible during this bull run. Decentralized video web-based is a highly encouraging use case and an innovation that video web-based service providers will require, regardless of whether they require it or not. The online video market is expanding at a rapid rate, and as platforms such as YouTube continue to impose restrictions on content creators, the demand for a practical, high-quality real-time video platform will only increase. I am betting on Theta. I assert that Theta is currently the leader in blockchain-based decentralized video web. In terms of development and reception, it has made unprecedented progress over the past year. Theta streamed arguably Coindesk's largest event ever. Theta collaborated with Google, which is a current member of the Theta organization. Theta.tv launched on more than 75 million Samsung mobile devices. Theta signed a contract with MGM Studios and endorsed Fail Army as their first premium content creator. Similarly, Theta joined forces with Changling to eliminate these inane YouTube crypto tactics. Theta enabled websites to embed Theta.tv streams and earn digital currency. Edgecast, the first completely decentralized online video platform, was launched by Theta. Theta obtained the first blockchain patent in the United States for a decentralized streaming convention. The Theta network has more than 3,000 organization hubs distributed across the globe, and it currently has smart contracts that are compatible with Ethereum and a web wallet module, paving the way for DeFi. Theta's 3.0 primary net is imminent, with ideal timing for the digital currency market's upward trend. The price activity of the Theta token has consequently skyrocketed and is looking steadily more certain. The T-fuel token is also siphoning, despite the fact that its tokenomics are dreadful.

Smart Contract Cryptocurrency Investment

You may examine digital currency prices and rankings multiple times per day. No matter how frequently I monitor these leaderboards, I am always surprised to discover an altcoin that was hidden by not really trying to hide. Heavenly is unquestionably one of these altcoins, and the recent price activity of its Lumens currency has shocked the crypto community. This is partially due to the fact that Stellar has been relatively under the radar compared to other crypto initiatives. When inquiring as to why XLM appears to be headed toward new all-time highs, there is no other explanation besides a positively trending market. However, what have I told you is that the actual response to the Stellar presentation of Stellar is much greater than you might have anticipated. In this section, I will explain Stellar's history, where it's headed, and how it may very well alter the digital currency landscape forever. Heavenly is a smart contract digital currency designed for a specific purpose: the exchange of significant value. This includes the exchange of tokenized resources such as Stellar's local Lumens currency, which trades under the ticker XLM. Stellar, unlike other crypto projects, is not endeavoring to replace the current monetary system. In any case, it's attempting to coordinate with it and improve payment channels between entities such as Central Banks. In a manner that would seem natural to Stellar, it requires all of the world's monetary frameworks to collaborate on a single organization. This has led to the recognition of Stellar as a financial coin alongside Ripple, and Stellar is a fork of Ripple. Jed Mccaleb, co-founder of Stellar and creator of the now-defunct MT. Gox digital currency exchange, was instrumental in establishing Swell. Mccaleb is a well-known figure in the crypto-currency industry. Jed had numerous ideas for Ripple that Ripple's governing body would not implement.

After repeatedly clashing with the directorate and other high-ranking staff, Jed departed Ripple in 2014 and began working for Stellar. While there are numerous similarities between Ripple and Stellar, the most significant difference is that Ripple is corporate, unified, and for benefit, whereas Stellar is anticipated to be public, decentralized, and non-benefit. This ethos is carried out by the Stellar development establishment, a California-based non-profit organization that creates Stellar. I will also mention that Ripple and Stellar are not in the greatest of health. In addition, as a prominent Ripple supporter, Jed received 9.5 billion XRP and still possesses approximately 4 billion XRP. Despite the fact that he is evidently bound by law to refrain from selling his XRP, this has made some XRP more valuable.

Since he departed Ripple, his transactions involving XRP have routinely made headlines and made XRP holders anxious. However, this is not the only reason Stellar has been in the news recently. In March of 2019, former mozilla CEO Danelle Dixon assumed the position of CEO at the Stellar enhancement organization. Not until two months later did Danelle detail the new direction Stellar would take. She explained that while Stellar would continue to focus on innovation and decentralization, it would increase its market initiatives and biological system development. In any case, this advertising and development would not be directed at those in the cryptocurrency space. It would be equipped for financial institutions and controllers that Stellar wishes to attract to the greatest extent possible. Stellar announced in September that its network of validators would be able to vote to limit the annual growth of Lumens. Validators voted for the proposition, and XLM expansion was removed from the October convention 12 update. Initially, XLM grew at a rate of one percent per year. This decision to have expansion despite the fact that validators on the Stellar network do not typically acquire mining rewards was rather peculiar. Instead, they are promoted to demonstrate the organization's benefits to them. Therefore, the vast majority of Stellar validator centers are corporate substances, which is Stellar's target market. Moreover, approximately 80% of XLM's initial supply of 100 billion was designated to the Stellar development organization, indicating that they were the ones most affected by this annual growth rate. In addition to refocusing on XLM expansion, Stellar consumed more than 55 billion XLM in November and redistributed the remaining 30 billion XLM to marketing, customer acquisition, and other expansionary initiatives. Despite the fact that the consumption represented more than half of XLM's total inventory, it had little impact on price. This is due to the fact that none of the available XLM at that time had been burned. Stellar's adjustment in token economics and orientation appears to have been profitable. By the end of 2019, the Stellar group had grown from 11 to 56 members. Danelle had begun to make progress with administrators in Washington, DC, the number of XLM accounts had multiplied, and the number of Stellar organization validators had increased by a factor of five. This takes us through 2020. Stellar has experienced an extremely busy year in 2020. In February, Stellar completely upgraded their website to make it more user-friendly. They also release their command, which provides an incredibly detailed summary of how they're spending their 30 billion XLM and even displays the current balances of their various accounts. Then in April Stellar formed an alliance with

Wells Fargo supports the blockchain examination firm Elliptic. The purpose of this organization is to ensure that all organizations utilizing Stellar, including digital currency exchanges, adhere to the monetary laws and regulations of their respective nations. At the May event where the agreement was disseminated,

Danelle explained that Stellar appears to be the blockchain on which Central Banks will build their Central Bank advanced monetary standards over the next five years. Almost every major government on the planet wants to implement a CBDC within the next few years, and they are turning to stable coin companies for assistance in developing the technology, while also looking to the crypto space for blockchains on which to build their CBDCs. As a part of its convention 13 overhaul, Stellar introduced in June a feature that many refer to as fine granularity control. This made it possible to prevent Stellar-based accounts from participating in transactions that violate financial regulations. This would make it extraordinarily straightforward to implement FinCEN's new proposal to require KYC for every advanced exchange, including those exceeding $250. In September, Danelle spoke about blockchain at a virtual event organized by the United States House Financial Services Committee. In it, Dannell displayed the various government-issued currencies tokenized on Stellar by institutions in countries such as Mexico, Argentina, Brazil, and Nigeria. Additionally, she emphasized the use of KYC in Stellar's institutional endeavors in general. The Circle Consortium then announced in October that the USDC stablecoin would be launched on the Stellar network in January 2021. That very month, Danele served as an expert for the IMF's online event concerning cross-line payments. Stellar released a video at the end of the month that evaluated their accomplishments during the second-to-last quarter of 2020. These included cultivating relationships with the international monetary discussion, which they have been doing since July. According to the video update, Stellar had more than twenty-five meetings with the world financial discussion, the OCC, and other public and global monetary bodies in the third quarter alone. Heavenly will also ostensibly play a significant role in the fourth modern upheaval, which is a crucial component of the global economic reset. In conclusion, Stellar's annual meridian event featured the director of blockchain and digital currency for the international monetary fund alongside the previous leader of the World Bank. This is significant, but it makes one question how it might impact the Lumens digital currency. Taking everything into account, I am bullish on XLM. Initially, all Stellar organization transactions are paid for with XLM. As a result of Stellar's adaptability to every customer's needs

In terms of being the blockchain for cross-border payments and Cbdcs, they have gained ground against every financial institution they encounter. Since Danelle became CEO, Heavenly has made inconceivable strides in reception, and all banks, businesses, and governments utilizing Stellar today and tomorrow will pay fees in XLM. In addition, it appears that USDC is gaining popularity among major financial institutions. It was recently reported, for instance, that Visa would coordinate USDC in its installments network with more than 60 million transporters. And all USDC sent on Stellar will incur an expense in Lumens, regardless of their value. In addition, Stellar's decision to modify the tokenomics of XLM by eliminating expansion and consuming the majority of its stock suggests that the company hopes to increase XLM's value. Logic dictates that the Stellar organization should compete for a larger sum of money as XLM increases in value. I am aware that Stellar's validator hubs voted in favor of this change in tokenomics, but considering that the vast majority of these validators are employed by the Stellar establishment and the very heritage organizations that they are in bed with, it is not a majority rule government. That brings me to my next point. Despite the fact that I am extremely bullish on the short- to medium-term price of XLM, it is not a cryptocurrency I am completely comfortable with in the long run. With each step closer to the Stellar convention, XLM bearers appear to be gaining less and less independence from the rat race. Stellar is inching closer and closer to the exact same monetary foundations that digital currency should supplant. This as well as Stellar is catering to delegated global organizations that do not appear to care about our fundamental wellbeing. Therefore, why would I support such an endeavor by holding their funds? Indeed, I invested in altcoins with smaller market caps for the same reason: to accumulate Satoshis. Overall, it appears that semi-controlled computerized monetary forms are on the horizon, and the only way we can truly secure our wealth is by investing in digital currencies we know and trust. Using the promotion surrounding financier currencies such as XLM is, in my opinion, a good way to accomplish this. We can without much of a stretch distinguish between the immediate and medium-term tokenomics and the longer-term goals of the Stellar development organization. One can appreciate the promise of Stellar technology to revolutionize global payments while also being concerned about the standards it adheres to. To conclude, I must provide my interpretation of what I believe will occur with Stellar in the coming years. I believe Stellar will continue to enjoy success in its partnerships with governments, financial institutions, and peripheral organizations.

global connections. I believe that many CBDCs will be founded on Stellar. I believe Stellar will continue to adjust its tokenomics and client authorizations to appease its partners and controllers. Nevertheless, I do anticipate that Stellar will face considerable opposition from the crypto community at that time. Why? Stellar has complied with the fact that a large number of other cryptographic money projects are working tirelessly to create truly decentralized platforms that will replace the incorporated secrecy, while Stellar is occupied with obedient executives and government officials. It is inevitable that a digital currency like

Bitcoin or Ethereum will become excessively large or too powerful to close. I believe the likelihood of this occurrence is significantly greater than what incorporated specialists would have you believe. Unquestionably greater than the possibility of the global monetary discussion or IMF coordinating their efforts to eliminate the authoritarian monetary frameworks they favor. When that time comes, broker currencies like Stellar may become obsolete because they never truly serve the interests of the average person. You could argue that some level of regulation and consistency in the digital currency space is necessary, and I concur. However, I also believe that there should be a middle ground, and Stellar appears to be firmly aligned with the current state of affairs, and thus is not the middle ground. On the bright side, there is a type of safeguard that is pre-programmed into federated frameworks, and that is that as power becomes more concentrated in the hands of the few, the price for breaching positions and mobilizing the many will increase. In my opinion, this is what has made cryptographic currency so successful. Cryptographic currency exists outside of the monetary system. It is a departure from a centralized financial framework where power is held by a small number of individuals, partnerships, and organizations. Assuming these frameworks were excellent, Bitcoin could never have been conceived, and even if it had, no one would have seen the need for it and it would have been obscured by obscurity. However, as the existing monetary system becomes increasingly corrupt and unstable, this demand will continue to grow. It's a disgrace that Stellar doesn't appear to recognize this, but perhaps they do and are merely cooperating until the time comes to confound a multitude of large institutions. Heavenly has accomplished a great deal in the past year. Since Danelle Dixon's appointment as CEO of the Stellar development organization in 2019, Stellar has expanded at an astounding rate with each step. Changes to XLM's tokenomics and designations, as well as a shift in the project's perspective, have been scheduled for the current calendar year. Stellar has five employees as of the beginning of 2021.

It was many times larger and had caught the attention of major actors in and outside of the digital currency space. In any case, as time passed, it became evident that Stellar's allegiance was to the current financial framework and not the cryptocurrency sector. The Stellar development organization's clear fixation on different three-letter associations that look to expand their control over the existences accomplishment in stressing, elements like the discussion OCC and others is worrying, yet it paints a promising picture of the future cost action of Lumens, which self-control each of the exchanges being sent by and between clients. Stable currencies and Central Bank electronic monetary standards appear to be Stellar's bread and butter, and the title of global payments processor could be theirs to claim. Any investments in XLM should be made with the understanding that XLM is an organization that has been progressively transferred into the hands of such individuals, which genuine digital currencies seek to depose. Stellar will likely face difficulties as digital currency initiatives emerge from the web's ether to wage war against the financial framework Stellar has adopted. Regardless, it will be an incredible ride, and if the world isn't already watching Stellar, you can bet that they will be shortly.

was discovered through various

Apparently favored consistency and

pertaining to others. While their IMF global economic

www.ingramcontent.com/pod-product-compliance
Lightning Source LLC
Chambersburg PA
CBHW050418120526
44590CB00015B/2007